Walking by Inner Vision

Stories & Poems

Lynda McKinney Lambert

To Sharon   Romans 8

Lynda McKinney Lambert

DLD Books

ISBN: 1543121624
ISBN–13: 978-1543121629

Dedication

I dedicate this book to the memory of my parents:
William Joseph McKinney (1916—1988)
Esther Luella Kirker McKinney (1920—2007)

Bill & Esther McKinney with Lynda, 1943

Start children off in the way they should go, and even when
they are old they will not turn from it.
—Proverbs 22:6 (NIV)

Table of Contents

Prologue

In Which I Knit a Life Back Together

In my earliest memories, knitting with two needles in my hands and a supple, colorful ball of yarn seemed to come naturally to me. Combine that activity with a quiet and sunny room, a comforting chair, and solitude, and I have a perfect day. Winter days cause me to remember a time when the possibility of ever knitting again seemed as far away as a distant star.

Knitting was something I learned as a young child. I taught myself how to knit by looking at an instruction book and by visiting a local merchant who gave me assistance.

No one in my family knitted. To this day, I have no idea how I ever became so absorbed in knitting, but it has been a lifelong passion.

It's been nearly a decade since I lost most of my eyesight due to a stroke–like event that killed my optic nerves. This condition is called Ischemic Optic Neuropathy; there was no way to predict this would happen and no treatment once it did its damage.

Since I did not know anyone who had profound sight loss, this unexpected challenge was disorienting for a few months as I tried to figure out what to do next. I thought my life was over, since I could do nothing I had done previously.

In the beginning, I did not know if it was day or night. The simplest tasks were impossible. I had so many unspoken questions:

How to cut my nails?

How to get toothpaste on my toothbrush?

How to apply makeup?

How to make a cup of tea?

How to make a phone call?

How to even find a phone number?

How to know what day it was, and how to make an appointment on a calendar?

How to memorize everything I would need to remember?

How to use a computer?

The strain of trying to see and the constant failures in doing ordinary activities overwhelmed me. I felt useless, and one morning I very quietly cried as I prayed out loud, "Oh, God. This is not how I want to spend my life!" There were no more words I could say. I was heartbroken.

Like many people with blindness, I suffered from painful headaches. I learned that these are "bad eye days." The entire body is affected by the brain straining to see. I was intensely aware of the connection between the brain and the body. My brain would try to see, but my body could not do the work of "seeing" any longer. This would be similar to a camera that is set on automatic focus, and if the camera is not able to focus, it just keeps on trying to do it. It's exhausting! Like the camera, my eyes were malfunctioning. When a bad eye day began, it would often mean another three days or so of intense pain. I spent many days in bed trying to cope. Bad eye days are now a part of my normal life, and I have learned to stop what I am trying to do: I rest and wait it out.

One dismal winter afternoon, I sat in the reclining chair. My feet were extended on the footrest and my eyes were closed. I often sit with my eyes closed, since it helps me to relax and center myself. I was thinking about the sweaters I made for needy children through a charity and wondering how I would ever make a sweater again. I thought of the sweater I was making at the time of my sudden sight loss. I longed to finish the sweater. Desire to complete this little child's sweater filled me, and I decided to pick up the unfinished project and give it a try.

I sat there with the yarn in my hands and held my needles tentatively. I could not even see the color of the yarn and certainly could not see the stitches or the needles. My eyes stared downwards, straining to see, but I could not.

I began by holding the yarn strand in place in my two hands. Just the feel of the yarn brought a surge of pleasure. The long, aluminum knitting needles felt cool against my warm hands. I remembered how much I had always loved to knit. If nothing else in my life was going right, I always had my knitting. *Can I ever do this again?* I wondered.

I started very slowly, moving the needles and trying to get them to balance. I shifted them between my two hands and put them into my normal knitting position. My breathing became shallow as I struggled. I tried to begin, stopped, and tried once again for the familiar feel of yarn and needles, now so strange and clumsy. I felt awkward, my needles now complete strangers.

I simply could not do it. I felt worthless, my hands exhausted and heavy. Were these the same hands that had been so nimble and flexible my whole life? How could this be?

Suddenly, I had a slight, faltering revelation, something I had not thought about before: I could not do it because I was trying to *see* it.

The idea came to me like a gentle whisper in my soul. It felt like a patient voice telling me, "Since you cannot see, you should just close your eyes and try to begin to feel it with your hands. Let your hands be your eyes now."

How ironic, I thought. *My desire to see what I am doing is preventing me from "seeing."*

I seemed to understand at this point that I must now learn to see non-visually. Intuitively, I knew I needed to use my hands and fingers combined with my other senses. My fingers would now become my eyes! And I thought, *Yes, instead of looking with two eyes, I can now look with ten fingers!*

Soon, I was feeling my way through this task. I finished that sweater and donated it to the charity that provided sweaters for needy children. God had allowed my passion for knitting to become my breakthrough in healing, and knitting again was the beginning step on the path to recovery.

Shortly after this healing breakthrough, I was able to attend a rehab center, where I further developed my personal adjustment to blindness. Of course, I took my knitting along with me.

I knitted my way through the hard days of struggles and the depression of trying to relearn how to do little ordinary activities that people take for granted. I learned how to put my knitting patterns onto a digital sound device called a Milestone. Oh, how I love this little device! With my Milestone, I can carry the verbal directions with me and I can knit anywhere.

I learned how to put my patterns on a computer so that I could read them again with adaptive technologies. I learned how to organize my knitting patterns in ways that I could access when I needed them. When I felt overwhelmed and tired from all the learning that I had to do each day, I retreated to my room and picked up my knitting. It was knitting that brought me through those hard times.

By successfully knitting again, I gained confidence in myself and took pride in what I could do instead of lamenting my losses. For me, knitting was a game changer. I was back in the game of knitting together a life. Manipulating the needles and yarn gave me pride deep down in my creative soul.

When someone stops me and compliments me on a beautiful sweater or stunning jacket I am wearing, I give them a wide smile and say, "Oh, thanks! I knitted it."

Eventually, I gained confidence in myself. One of my greatest pleasures these days is to attend a knitting group, where I can sit in a circle with other women who love to knit. I continue to experience the healing power of knitting as I stretch myself to do projects that are beautiful and satisfying. With each new knitting project completed, I gain confidence and pride in regained skills. It has not been a path with no more challenges. I still struggle to do things that were once so easy for me to do in my knitting. But I see it now as my relationship with Jesus, a lifetime of learning to trust Him to bring me to the place I need to be, despite the obstacles we encounter. Friends in my knitting group see me struggling, and I sometimes become frustrated with my errors and the many times when I have to rip it all out and begin again. I say to them, "Knitting keeps me humble and constantly reminds me I need help." With God's grace and faith in His guidance, I am learning to walk by faith and not by sight as I knit my life back together again.

JANUARY

January Scene

Dull morning light
blurs the overview
rows of mailboxes
rusty red and gray–green
weathered metal.
Across the street
bare maple branches grasp
curled leaves trapped in wintry spines
like a wet umbrella, partly opened.
My body aches
moving slowly beneath
golden silk blankets
where two lovers slept
entwined throughout
a frigid January night.
Sheltering pines
embrace the neighborhood
a yellow house lurks
behind ancient spruce trees
nearly twice its height
a burnt–orange house broods

in the distance
between limbs of naked maple trees.
We listen
for the next
winter snowfall
wait
for its silent passage
along the banks of
the icy river.

A January State of Mind

January is a confusing month!

Do you feel stretched in two different directions? Strange, because I feel like I am two different persons. One is the public image, the forward–looking face I wear most of the time. She is the go–getter, the high achiever, the bold, fearless professional woman. Yet at different times, you can see the other face, another me. She is often unusually quiet, private, occasionally uncertain, aloof at times, and not always much of a group person. This brings me to a deeper question. "Do we experience duality because January is on our minds?" I do have these mixed and competing thoughts in January every year. Do you?

Have you ever scanned back through your own previous January entries in your journals? January is a great month for reflection. Some scrutiny will give you additional insight into what you were thinking about at that time.

Another way is to look back over your calendar from last January. This might help you get some insight into your activities for the month.

I feel like I am doing a circular dance of duality.

Centrifugal movements urge me to move outward, or onward, while conflicting, centripetal powers are demanding me to move inwards—all at the same moment. The result is that I am at a standstill and cannot move in any direction. I'm stuck! The tensions must be the two sides of me. There's something hidden deep inside of us that makes us restless, uncertain, and hesitant, in spite of all our best efforts to make changes for the year ahead. Is it possible that while we are looking forward for the new horizons in our life, at the same time we are looking backwards?

Perhaps! In January, we can gain wisdom and reconnect with something spectacular that we missed because we were too close to it to really see it!

The ancient Romans named the months in their year after their pagan gods. They had only ten months in their year and did not have the two months we know as January (Januarius) and February (Februarius). These two months were added to the Roman year circa 700 BCE. January was named after their god Janus.

Unlike our calendar today, January was not the first month of the Roman year until after Numa Pompilius, the second king of Rome, changed the sequence of the months into the twelve–month calendar. To the Roman mind, an odd number was considered to be lucky. For this reason, the king changed the number of days in several months from the unlucky even numbers to the lucky odd numbers. Long after this change from a ten–month to a twelve–month calendar, the emperor Julius Caesar made additional changes. After 46 BCE, February was designated the month which could make up a "leap year," and additional changes were made. Instead of the Roman calendar, it was now called the Julian calendar.

Maybe the dual feelings we are having on this first month of the year is because it is named in honor of Janus. Naming is so important. Our name has helped us to develop into the person we are today, even though we were unaware of that most of the time. Experts recommend that families carefully consider what they will name an unborn child. They caution us to choose a name that will be a positive influence on a child, because the child will grow into the various aspects of the name's meaning. I often pause to be grateful to my parents for giving me a name that means "beautiful." It makes me smile every time I think of it. I appreciate my name, and I'm reminded I want to live up to its traditional meaning.

In Roman and Greek mythology, the gods and goddesses in the pantheon have different functions or jobs. Janus is the god who guards and controls gates and doorways. I envision his job as that of the one who orchestrates migrations and journeys.

As a Christian, I know that only God is the One who controls my gates and doorways. Because of this fact, I am thinking of January as a doorway or gate into a new beginning with fresh, exciting expectations. In my personal life, January is a gateway to pass through into a new beginning.

I love to travel and visit new places, to learn about interesting things I enjoy. I'd like my personal path for this New Year to include some type of travel. It could be that

God's will for me this year is to help me move through a passageway to arrive at a place of new opportunities or challenges. In reality, I know that each of us will travel from one place to another in the next year. We often say, "That's life!" But more than that, our circumstances are an inner voyage or personal transfer of some sort. Sensations of discontent and uncertainty are only natural as we realize the impact of January.

I often think of my life as a passage from one place, left behind, to the new place, just ahead of me. I searched for those pathways in my poems, journal entries, and dreams. This recurring theme develops in my writing projects as I write about being in one place, yet longing to go to another place, or back to where I used to be. I view my life journey as a pilgrimage—and I believe we can all see different kinds of personal journeys in our recollections.

The poet Matsumo Basho expressed such thoughts in his book *The Narrow Road to the Interior*. He wrote: "The past remains hidden in clouds of memory. Still it returned us to memories from a thousand years before. Such a moment is a reason for a Pilgrimage."

For the ancient Romans, January was the festival month for Janus. He is depicted in artworks as standing in the doorway. But the problem is that Janus has two faces! Simultaneously, he looks forward through the doorway to the passage ahead with one of his faces, while the other face looks backwards. One face to the front. One face to the rear! Here is the dual message that we encounter if we do not know which way we are facing at the beginning of the year. It's a problem that has been with humankind since the time when Adam and Eve had to leave the Garden. Is it any wonder we feel so uncertain in January? Sometimes we don't know if we are coming or going through Janus's passageway.

On the other hand, Jesus also spoke about standing at a door. His message was clear, and we can be certain that when Jesus stood at the door and knocked, He was looking directly at us. His invitation to open the door and let Him into our hearts is recorded in Revelation 3:20.

If we do not personally know Jesus as our Savior, we will be like Janus. We want to go forward; another part of us looks backwards. I've stepped right into Janus's vision myself at times. That is when we become confused and uncertain and feel like we are going in two directions at one time.

When we choose to look only to Jesus, we will look forward, asking Him to help us set our intentions into the pathway where He will be walking with us for the New Year. But what I feel rumbling inside of my being is the reminders of a backwards step at the same time. I often wonder why I don't recognize, or put into language, what I am really experiencing internally in January.

Is it because the noisy crowd drowns out our inner life, inner feelings, intuitions, and our internal voice? They shout out, "Happy New Year." We have been told this is the time for our expectations to be declared and realized—yet there is that other side of Janus in our mind. As we ride the crest of January, the pinnacle of the New Year, we have expectations for what we believe the New Year holds for us. Those are the thoughts we talk about with others.

Here is what we often do not speak about, though. It's just too hard to put into words, sometimes, because it's painful.

We have an inner critic, an unseen voice reminding us of past failures, deflated expectations, shortcomings, blunders, and more. That is the other side of Janus! Oh, we fail to understand this side, and we sure don't want to be talking about it to anyone. We have to keep up the smile, keep up with expectations. We have to... You fill in the blanks here.

It does not take much of a leap to see the self–centered, secular expectations of our contemporary culture. The New Year resolutions madness can literally paralyze anything creative, inspired, spiritual, artistic, resourceful, inventive, imaginative, intuitive, innovative, and productive inside us. The Janus masks, facing in two directions at the same time, are in place for so many people who will never experience inner peace and joy because they are running so fast in a direction that will lead them to emptiness, after all.

But there is a way out of this predicament. Stop and be quiet for a little while. Maybe get up early tomorrow morning, when the house is still. Spend fifteen minutes in silence. Keep your thoughts focused on getting in touch with God. Let Him direct you to your purpose in life. In a quiet time, we can turn off the loud voices that distract us so easily and cause us to be confused. God is there, in the still, small voice, waiting for you.

Contemporary culture tells us to be determined to do what we want to do, to push our way to the top of whatever we decide to do. The clamoring voices are loud and demanding, often brightly colored, cutout images of what we should look like and how we should think. They shout to us about how strong we are, how we need to be "empowered" so we can do anything we want to do. The crowd says we need to call ourselves powerful and smart.

Oh, but wait a minute! Stop for a moment; listen for the gentle whisper of your inner being. Listen.

We can look forward with expectations that are grounded in divine purpose for our life.

I recommend a look back because it is wholesome for us to do. History bears fruit, you know. We bear fruit as we discipline our mind to study history. Our life's personal story is like a display of artworks on a gallery wall. The images are displayed. If we are careful and honest when we look at the pictures of our own thoughts, we'll find some gems as well as some clinkers. Both are good for us to consider, because they all show us the path we are on.

January is a state of mind.

The Other Side of the Mountain

Do you remember the little song about a bear that went over a mountain to see what he could see? You probably learned it as a child. I did! At the beginning of a new year, I remembered this song.

"The bear goes over the mountain, to see what he can see."

I envision the New Year as a view from the top of a mountain where I arrive at the completion of the last year. I get a glimpse into a fresh new beginning.

From this lofty vantage point, inner vision allows me to imagine new dreams.

I foresee stories I've gathered my entire life. The top of the mountain is a crossroads where I can inquire, *Where do I go from here?*

We most likely will not have a clear direction initially but will decide to take a step. Intention begins the moment we decide to take action.

Whatever the day brings, we have a choice in how we will think and act. Choose to keep your mind on activities that delight and inspire you as well as others you encounter each day.

Write your INTENTIONS out and keep them in your mind. Here, at the top of the mountain of the New Year, we have a fresh new view on the other side of the mountain. Decide where you will go from here. You can create the view you see ahead as you gaze off in the distance.

How can we determine what our INTENTIONS will be?

Let's begin with ONLY ONE simple question:

Who will I be this year?

In the mornings, I like to say out loud, "What will you have me do today, Lord?" Think about your lifestyle, gifts, and talents and jot them down. What do YOU have to share? Everyone has something to give.

As I look out over the mountaintop in my own life, I intend to be walking on the high road. I'll stop to ask, *Is this the high road?* This question will help me make better decisions in whatever I am doing. I will keep on going because it brings wonderful surprises and unexpected gifts we never knew we possessed. I know that when we keep on giving out our love and goodness, it does return back to us in ways we never envisioned.

How about YOU?

What path will you choose to walk on?

Here are my top three intentions for my own future.

1. I INTEND to spend some time in intentional silence, rest, and prayer each day. I'll make a quiet place in my home where my creative spirit can rest, gather new ideas, and find inspiration. This will be my first priority of each new day.

2. I INTEND to read some of the classic books and focus on the wisdom of the writers and philosophers who left behind some of the greatest ideas. I want to discover how those thoughts from the past have influenced me in contemporary times.

3. I INTEND to continue writing my two blogs and keeping up with my website. I'll look over them and select my best work for upcoming projects in the new year.

You see, it does not have to be some grand scheme that helps you set your intentions. It can be in the mundane and often overlooked details of your daily routine. My intentions are not grand designs; they are simple, ordinary activities I can do, and they fit in with my personal gifts and interests. Each of the three I mentioned here will help me with my creative life.

Now, it's your turn! You will have your own set of intentions. Your list will most likely not be anything like mine. Just be yourself and write out some INTENTIONS that will fit into your own lifestyle for this year! Consider what you will discover on the other side of the mountain. What do you see?

FEBRUARY

Sunday Morning in Winter

A cool breeze
wraps my bare feet
like a gray cashmere robe.
My own reflection
on a clear glass
surface
slowly revealed.
Outside the window
an icicle border
surrounds
the aging Douglas fir.
Quick movements
in the shadow
reveal
one small ruffled bird
on snow–clogged branches.
Today
words wait
to be written
in spite of the cold.

Lynda's Story: Vision and Revision

To view work as a pilgrimage is to put our heart's desires to hazard because merely by setting out, we have told ourselves that there is something bigger and better, or even smaller and better—above all something more life giving—that awaits us in our work, and we are going to seek it. We look around to see what we have for the journey and find at bottom that we possess only intuitions and imagination....
—From *Crossing the Unknown Sea*, by David Whyte

We know from the beginning of our lives, before we have words, that we are creators. I cannot remember a moment in my life when I was unaware of my creative instincts, abilities, and intuition. I've always had an active inner life that guides me.

When working in my studio, I concentrate on creating a body of work. This method of production keeps me focused, because I am always creating a collection that will have a unified appearance when viewed in a gallery exhibition. But arriving at the place where an artist can create a unified body of work may take many years. It is a benchmark that can be seen; it separates a hobbyist from a professional.

Insight into my own work developed over a long period of time as I pursued two degrees in painting (BFA and MFA) and an MA in English. Those degrees are rigorous and intense fields of pursuit. The years of higher education accomplishments gave me a professional mindset; it required that I ask the difficult questions during the process. With the passage of time, I discovered who I am and what my intentions are in my work.

Some questions always come up in any conversation with people who are not artists.

When does the creative process begin?
Where do ideas come from?
How do you know when your work is finished?
Who can learn to make art or write poems?

I recognize some clear steps in the development of my artwork and my writing. There is no separation between the two, in my experience. I believe the same about artificial separations between sacred and secular. There are none!

First, I often spend time in contemplation, where I focus my thoughts on a particular word, phrase, theme, or image. Something keeps recurring to me, often subconsciously. Awake or asleep, I experience this something moving around inside my mind. My thoughts keep going back to that little bit of insight I am feeling. I see it in visions when awake, in dreams when asleep. At first, it can be elusive as I begin to dwell on it. This first step may take months or even years. Initially, though, I am just aware of something that I cannot put into words. This beginning stage is a concept, initially, not something I can see visually with my eyes. It is far deeper than that. It's known as intuition, and every human person has been given this gift of knowing. It is in our gut.

Everything, for me, comes from fragments. I never see more than a fragment of an idea or a thought before I begin the creative work. It's the same for me when I am writing or when I am making an artwork. An object, story, poem— all made by grasping onto a shifting, moving notion of a fragment. Eventually, these shards, little pieces, and musings lead to the beginning of a new work. Before I ever begin the actual labor of creating the art or the story, I feel like I have encountered a labyrinth. At the entrance of this maze, I am a willing participant, although I never know where I will be taken. I step into the doorway or passage into the labyrinth. The pilgrimage begins now! I do not have a roadmap or a clearly designated destination when I step out to begin this journey.

The second step is the preparation of the physical space. At this point, I have a keen sense that I am about to depart on a private, solitary voyage. I begin the excursion by organizing and clearing the clutter from my studio or office. If I am writing, my office has to be put in order first. If I am beginning to make art, the studio must be well organized, clean, and clutter–free. I cannot tolerate any kind of disorder. I call this stage "organizing the chaos."

Third, I assemble the materials for the new projects. At this time, I make decisions about the types of materials I'll use. Beads, fabrics, paints, found objects, and natural gemstones are gathered for an artwork. I do the same when writing. I collect images, ideas, themes, and words that I might want to use while writing. I often feel like a florist selecting the flowers and plants for my next bouquet. This is one of the most exciting parts of my process!

Fourth, I am now ready to depart on the journey. The work in progress feels like a dance, and I seldom know in advance just where this tango will eventually lead. What I do know is that I'm embarking on another new path. It's like I arrived at the top of a mountain and I am looking over into the territory just beyond where I stand. I am energized and ready to go. Despite these conscious steps of preparation, the process I use is intuitive; there are no rules. I am completely free and anxious to begin. I think, *Is there any other profession in life where there are no rules? No wrong way to do anything? No mistakes and no accidents? Where else in our lives can we be free and have no expectations placed on us by anyone?*

A handwritten sign on my office wall reminds me:

Trust Inner Feelings

Harbingers

"I saw a robin this morning. The bird was in my back yard. Spring is here!"

Every year in late February, an announcement similar to this one is published in our small-town newspaper. By late February, local residents begin to report the first sighting of a red-breasted robin, a harbinger of spring. Typically, this will be when people begin to get excited as they start thinking about spring.

For residents who walk outside on wintry days, it's a different story. It's not so unusual, because people can see an occasional robin all through the winter months if they are alert and watching for the birds. Even the robins are safely hidden away, keeping warm in the thick evergreen branches of pine trees and bushes.

The belief that all robins fly south for the winter is an old wives' tale, a commonly believed myth handed down for centuries. It's not quite true. Most people believe the robins will come back here to western Pennsylvania just in time for spring. The robins become a harbinger of spring, among a number of other stories about animals who predict changing seasons, solar or lunar phases, and weather.

In the stillness of the late–winter woods, my dogs and I listen for robins to sing out melodious, lyrical songs. Red–breasted robins, in fact, are resident birds in some eastern states.

I live in a rural wooded area beside a winding creek in western Pennsylvania, and many of the robins stay right here, where they have shelter in the woods and fresh water in the brooks and streams. Beneath the melting snow, the birds find fresh worms and seeds in abundance on the floor of the meadows and woods.

The late–winter wonderland outside my window today conjures up all sorts of wintry tales in my imagination. My cat, Bessie, is curled up beneath my computer screen; she closed her eyes and drifted away in quiet contentment. As I begin to work on a new story, I glance over at her occasionally. Bessie's presence reminds me to consider the stories and experiences I have known about animals and their connection to the earth, the heavens, and the mythological tales from antiquity of the underworld. Decades of past seasons, of changes in our lives, and our winter remembrances arrive quietly with the new–falling snow. Yet the coldest season of the year is harsh and often feels like it's a time when we experience a period of cutting back, breaking apart, or taking away of everything we loved or desired. While it may seem that February is a month when everything remains frozen, dormant, or even dead, it simply isn't the case.

February is a month when gardeners do the hard pruning on a variety of plants and trees. An accomplished gardener will cut back the frozen branches at this time. The gardener wants the trees and bushes to grow well in the spring, and so he cuts them back near the end of winter. It seems odd, doesn't it? To have the desired growth in spring, the gardener makes a trek through the frozen landscape to prune his trees and shrubs. We don't usually associate pruning with wintertime. It seems backwards. It seems all wrong.

According to Chinese theory, there will always be opposing life forces in the universe. It is called "yin" and "yang," present in every season. "Yin" is the passive–negative force and "yang" is the opposing, active–positive force. Watch for the opposing forces at work in nature every day in all seasons. In fact, we can feel those forces at work inside our body and in our thoughts if we are sensitive and patient. There are opposing life forces in every living creature and in all of nature.

Perhaps that is why so many ancient myths have a focus on wintertime and on extraordinary creatures that have supernatural, divine origins and powers as they interact with humanity. These mythical animals bring predictions for the future in the lives of finite people.

In religious traditions of the early Europeans and Native Americans, we can find myriad animals that interact with humans. Such animals are known as totems. A totem holds transformative, sacred powers, and each person has her own personal totem animal. My totem is a crow. I say, "I am a Crow Spirit," and that carries a great deal of meaning for me. I am always aware of my totem, particularly when I am outside and walking in the woods. Crows surround me and call out; I call back to them. A person can find their totem through practice, or sometimes the totem animal actually finds the person instead. In my experience, crows found me. I encounter them daily on my walks, and I even see them when I am traveling a long distance from my home. Crows are ever-present to me. Historically, the crow (or raven) is a harbinger of a number of different conditions depending on the culture we are looking into. Mystical, powerful animals are present in all time periods.

A totem is a spirit helper, a harbinger, from the ancient past that comes to visit the person; the totem brings wisdom, healing, information, and insight into the future, visits in our dreams, gives us warnings and visions. Contemporary people around the world have beliefs about what is sacrosanct or what is secular. All generations have expressed longings for a sacred path via the legends of animals who are harbingers. I believe there is no division between sacred or secular—they are one. All of creation is sacred.

For example, there is a small mountain town in Pennsylvania called Punxsutawney. Here, an event is scheduled annually that involves an ordinary, native animal that has the ability to predict the end of winter and the beginning date of spring. The Pennsylvania Dutch legend dictates that Punxsutawney Phil will leave his groundhog burrow just before dawn on February 2nd, at exactly 7:28 a.m. Pennsylvania's world-famous groundhog is a favorite tourist attraction. The crowds gather to see a supernatural event that occurs on a frigid late-winter morning.

The president of the Groundhog Day Organization hoists plump, furry little Phil up into the air for all to see. Television cameras are rolling and reporters cover the show. Phil appears to whisper in the president's ear. The president translates Phil's message to the anxiously awaiting crowd. Of course, all of this is arranged by the committee in advance. No one cares about that! Everyone enjoys the event.

"Spring is right around the corner," the President shouts as the excited audience applauds. Everyone is happy.

You may recall a movie, *Groundhog Day*, which has a metaphysical theme with a cyclical world view. The film is often an assignment for college students who are studying modern or post-modern theory, and it's a good example of a collapsed linear timeline.

By the end of winter, Pennsylvania residents have usually had quite a bit of snow, zero temperatures, blustery winds, and hours of snow-shoveling. All of these activities, along with the gray days that seem endless, might begin to give people cabin fever. We start to become weary as we pass through the mundane days when sunshine is scarce for a few months. This is a yin and yang type of cycle in our lives. By this time, people are weary of winter and say they have cabin fever. It really means they are feeling depressed and are longing for sunshine.

Our stories of the solitude and desolation of winter

become the focus of our hopes as we anticipate the time of rejuvenation and resurrection. In anticipation of spring's arrival, we watch for the harbingers. We are no different than the ancients in our contemporary longings. We look for divination from the heavens. We want to be delivered from winter.

Phil said, "Spring is just around the corner."

We laughed with joy when we heard his message. We looked around and saw the robins sifting through the layer of snow to find some food. The gardener stood nearby with his cutting tools in hand. The hard pruning is complete. Spring is just around the corner.

Note: You can read more about Phil by going here: http://www.groundhog.org/

William's Red Roses

Early morning is my favorite time of day. My habit is to walk into the bathroom, pull up the blind, and peer outside to see what this new day is like. When I looked out the window early this morning, it was not yet daylight. The world was a soft, hazy, grayish blue. Snow! Newly fallen snow covered the earth like a pristine, frigid blanket. The wind was not blowing and the fresh day seemed eerily still. Even the early morning shrieks of black crows were absent. I glanced out over the wooded hillside, far beyond this second–story window. Everything was quiet. Subdued. Bleak.

A winter storm moved in yesterday, just as the weather reports predicted. By noon, the rural roads in our neighborhood were already covered with the kind of large snowflakes that quietly surrounded everything. There is something about the anticipation of a snowstorm that stirs us to remember our childhood.

"Oh, this is the perfect snowstorm! It's the kind of snowfall that I love," I shouted to my husband. "It's exactly the kind of crisp, cold winter day that makes me so excited. I feel like I am a little child when I see this snow," I continued to tell him. I admit I am nostalgic when snow brings layers of distant memories back to my mind. Memories of past years arrived with the snow. They are like a child's building blocks, tumbling down one over another. Thoughts of childhood mingled with the aromas in my mother's kitchen on distant winter days as I peered through the fogged–up windowpane.

On winter days, my mother often baked chocolate chip cookies, yeast breads, and pumpkin pies for the family. She knew her four children would be hungry when they came home from school in the late afternoon. We smelled the fragrances of her baking as we opened the back door into the kitchen.

In the early 1950s, my mother could have been one of the women in the magazine advertisements. She might have been Betty Crocker. She wore a freshly ironed cotton house dress as she cleaned, cooked, and sang hymns as she moved through the house. She had a clear alto voice and the people at church always requested that she sing something special in church on Sundays.

I have no memories of my mother wearing anything but a cotton dress every day. She wrapped a starched and ironed pastel gingham apron around her waist. The apron covered the front of her dress when she was cooking. Later, when I was in high school, she expanded her wardrobe and occasionally wore a pair of slacks.

We grew up knowing for sure that our mother was a lady. It had nothing to do with our humble economic status. Prior to the 1960s, a lady would never think of wearing anything but a dress every day to do her household chores and cooking for her family.

Yesterday, my own kitchen was warmer than usual. The room smelled like sweet, ripe, red cherries and spicy cinnamon. I opened the oven door a little at a time to let the hot, fragrant vapors escape and warm the room around me. I put on oven mitts, reached into the hot oven, and slowly, steadily, pulled out the piping–hot glass baking dish. This was the perfect day to bake a cherry crisp! Before it had a chance to cool, I dug a soup spoon deep into the cherry crisp and removed a little dish of the sweetness. I told myself, *Just a little taste!*

As I lifted the warm, red cherry delight to my mouth, I reflected on the snow outside the windows, noticing how it had accumulated on the old, weathered gray fence that surrounds the yard. The oak fence was built by my husband, our children, and some of their strong, male teenage friends in the summer of 1977. The fence surrounded the swimming pool built that spring. Every year since then, in springtime, the fence becomes the backdrop for the perennials when they begin to bloom.

Why is it that on solitary winter days, distant memories come calling?

Today, I felt transported to a particular sparkling day in August. It was my birthday; my father gave me a red rose bush in a black plastic container. Thin roots burst out from holes in the bottom of that container. I knew the rose bush desperately needed to be planted so it could thrive, but I was so young and busy taking care of my large family and didn't take the time to appreciate the gift. I did not plant it for a couple more years. This particular memory makes me feel so disappointed in myself. Because of my neglect, the bush did not flourish, and it did not bloom. A rose bush is meant to be planted by just such a fence as I had, so that it can bloom and twine upwards toward the morning light.

About fifty summers passed since my father gave me that red rose bush. Once it was finally nestled in the rich, dark earth next to the wooden fence, I never had the heart to dig it up, even though it never bloomed. I left it there as a reminder that time passes rapidly, and one day it is too late to say "thank you." Too late to appreciate some gifts we received when we were young. A dull sorrow always took root in my heart when I thought of that rose bush.

But as I watched the snow drifting this morning, onto the wooden fence, it unearthed more memories.

Last summer, I found something so unexpected out there on that old fence that I had to walk closer to have a better look. Could it possibly be what I was thinking it might be? Closer inspection revealed that the old rose bush my father gave me for my birthday so long ago was in full bloom! A joyous riot of deep red color wound all over the fence. The thorny, thick vine moved through the rough, weatherworn planks, from the inside of the fence to the outside. From every angle, the fully blooming roses could be seen. The tender tips of the branches reached upwards, far beyond the tops of the fence slats. It reached upwards, swaying in the sunlight of a balmy summer day. I stood entranced by those old–fashioned, deep–red roses. They were wide open, with soft crimson petals that fluttered outward. There was an inner crown of tiny little yellow pistils that looked like a circle of delicate yellow flowers surrounding the roses' centers.

My father's roses were blooming! In my great amazement, I said it out loud. "My father's red climbing roses are blooming! Oh, thank you, Dad!"

I thought about my father's birth name, William—an ancient name going back to the Teutonic ages. It's a strong name. A perfect name for a little boy who would be orphaned in childhood. A young husband who was drafted into WW II and would leave his wife and new baby girl to spend two years in freezing trenches during winter days in Europe. A hardworking father who would labor in the steel mills for a weekly paycheck to support the family he loved. A valiant man who gave the days and years of his life for the family and never expected anything in return. We learned the lessons of living a good life in the home he built for us with his own hands.

Names are important. Dad's Germanic name is Wilhelm. It can be broken down into two parts. "Will" means will or determination. "Helm" is a helmet. The two parts together mean "resolute protector." William, my father, desired to teach his children how to live an honorable life. In order to do that, he picked up his steel lunch bucket and safety helmet in the early morning when his children were still asleep in their beds. In the darkness of the morning, Dad left for his long walk down the railroad tracks and through the woods, and finally crossed over the creek on the wooden planks of a swinging bridge to eventually reach the entrance gate of the steel mill.

Today, I know that beneath the layer of snow, just in front of the weathered fence, there is a red rose bush waiting through the silence of the wintry weather.

Sunshine will come in the spring to warm the chilled earth. The red rose bush will begin to grow once again.

My husband has turned up the radio in the warm kitchen. He is listening to the radio. I walk into the kitchen and we embrace. My husband has a wide smile on his face. He tells me this is his favorite song. We dance together until the song ends.

Spring did arrive as it always does, but the winter months had been unusually harsh, and we lost many plants and trees during the icy storms. William's red roses never bloomed again.

My Daughter Cut the Roses

My daughter looked
at the bouquet of fresh roses
noticed two of them were drooping.
"Let me show you how to trim the roses
so they stay fresh and strong," she said.
Her hands held the roses tenderly
One–by–one, trimmed off extra leaves
"These will make the water stink," she said.
She found scissors in the drawer
put the roses in a bowl of tepid water
held each stem under water
sliced them all, diagonally—
"As I cut the rose under the water,
little bubbles of air come to the surface.
Now, when the rose inhales
it will only breathe water into it,
it won't fill up with air.
The living water inside the stems
gives longer life to each rose."
She carried the freshened flowers
In the tall glass vase

back to the center of the dining room table
darkest crimson buds, sunny yellow petals,
deep green fern leaves
and a frilly white carnation.

MARCH

March Arrived Like a Capricious Cat

Glass wind chimes
hang
immovable
stiff
shrouded in new snow
March arrived like a capricious cat
crouched—
hunkered down, bent over
spring–loaded, squat
Changeable!
Early this morning
I stepped cautiously through deep snow
March is the time to follow new dreams
that arrived in the flurry
of late winter snowstorms and blizzards
quietly
wordless
yet surging
inside, beneath layers of trees
my awakened
awareness heard songs

crows called
across the grey sky
sharp, staccato
lyrical melodies
red–breasted robins sang duets
together
hidden
somewhere beyond, out of sight
March arrived like a lion today
swept away my doubts.

In Which I Find Color in Late Winter

My husband, Bob, was still in bed this morning when I walked over to the window and opened the blinds. It was late morning. We were both happy to see that the entire winter landscape and sky appeared to have a bright blue hue washed all over it. The scene appeared as though a watercolor painter had mixed up a very thin wash of transparent blue hues and brushed the thin liquid paints all over a blank canvas. This surprising, brilliant landscape consisted of shades of turquoise, cerulean, azure, sapphire, and cobalt—every imaginable shade of blue was overlaid on the picture we viewed from our window. We were delighted with the delicate colors this particular morning gave us; it was an unexpected surprise of brilliant morning light today!

I know that as winter winds down to its end, we all begin to complain and lament the weather and dread the daily forecasts of storms and low temperatures. Some days, we seem to be in a deep freeze, with winter snow storms and squalls moving over the land like waves on an angry, stormy ocean.

The official designation of February and most of March is late winter. That's because it will be a while before spring is actually here.

We know spring will arrive on March 21st, but during the first months of the New Year, we often feel like the spring equinox is a long way off. But when we really take the time to look closely into what the days are like at this time of year, we will discover that winter days are colorful, and each new day holds a special beauty not found in any other months of the year.

Because we think about black ice, black branches, white snow, dismal, gray days, dark, moody clouds, crystal ice, or whiteouts, we choose to think that a winter landscape has only black, gray, and white hues. Yet a closer view reveals it's not a bleak, gray, black–and–white season at all. This time of year just has a different set of clothing than the other months and seasons. Look closer and find the subtle tints and effects in what appeared to be a stark landscape. Look for the tinges of warm colors in the shadows. Search the sky and see the delicate lilac and wispy green shades. There are even a lot of peachy strokes of color in the barren trees, if you look close enough. Every imaginable shape, form, and tinge of color in the spectrum is still present during winter, but you have to be looking for them. They are subtle and shy. Let's begin to give winter a break and appreciate all the myriad colors it has to share with us! Let's do a little project together and see what we can find in winter's magic palette.

Here's a nice project for you to begin working on. You

can create a photo essay in which you will observe the changes and shifts in colors. Discover the colors of late winter by yourself, or with a friend.

For our experiment, we will need a camera and a little bit of time to take some pictures of just one spot of landscape near where you live. This is the perfect month to begin your own photo essay of the colors in your own part of the world.

First: Select one piece of landscape that you like.

Take a few photos of this place. Now, in the seasons that will be coming along during the year, return to this exact spot and capture additional photos. Use the first snapshots you acquired to determine your exact location. Maybe a tree or bush or some sort of landmark will be your focus. This will help you create a cohesive view in all of the photos you will be taking during the year.

I chose to photograph my Zen Meditation Garden for this experiment. Bob created this unique Japanese garden a few years ago, and I love gazing at this peaceful garden in any season.

Second: After you select your location, jot down a note so you know where you were standing when you took your photos. Believe me, you will not remember your spot in the months ahead if you don't make a note of it. You want your photos to be as similar as possible for this experiment.

Third: In the months ahead, pay attention to the changing landscape in your photos. I think you will be amazed by what you will see in the progression of seasons, in the lighting, shadows, shifts, and changes.

Look for the relationship between the color changes in

your landscape photos. As you look at your pictures, be aware that we all have some preferences in colors we are particularly fond of. We think of specific colors for each season, and we even call the colors "spring colors," a "fall palette," and "sunny summer colors." Our minds are preset to expect particular colors for each different season. Look at the seasons with an open mind and a willingness to find some surprises.

Keep in mind that what we see will affect how we feel, because we humans are greatly influenced by our surroundings and light changes.

We associate colors with many words. For example, if I say "drab," you most likely think of a dirty gray or an olive green. If I mention "the Caribbean," you may think bright blue, orange, hot pink, etc.

The same is true for each season. Winter, spring, summer, and fall evoke a particular palette in our minds. Adjectives can evoke emotions, bring to mind sensations, and suggest powerful color preferences in our thoughts. There have been numerous scientific studies in which preferences and emotions are determined by the colors we see around us, as well as by spoken words.

Because the colors of winter remind us of the cold season, we might feel a shiver run through our body as we look at those photos, even if it's a summer day.

But I say, "Give winter a chance!" Look for the myriad hues that are there in the landscape, and you will find them. At first glance, the winter landscape seems to be barren, cold, and stark. But those are the emotions we are feeling and not the facts. Lay any negative or preconceived emotions aside for a moment, if you will, and look deeper into nature to find beauty in the rich colors of winter.

If you are visually impaired, as I am, then this can be a wonderful opportunity for you to partner with a sighted person. In doing it this way, the sighted person will also see the revelations that are found in the colors of winter. After the photos are completed, it would be a great project for you and your sighted partner to develop a nice scrap book of the changing colors of the seasons to share with other friends.

Another thing you can do is to have some of your photos scanned onto card stock and make the photos into cards for various seasons of the year. Your family and friends will be delighted with such a thoughtful gift. I am planning to create my own Christmas card this year. I'll scan in my favorite winter photo for the front of the card. For the inside, I will type in an original poem I wrote just for this special gift. In fact, I already have my poem ready for this project. This way, I am celebrating Christmas at the beginning months of the New Year. I'll have my surprise all ready to mail out when the time arrives in late autumn.

What other things can you do with the colors of winter?

In Like a Lion and Out Like a Lamb

March arrived this year like a CAPRICIOUS CAT—or a LION.

We've all heard that if March arrives like a lion, it will leave like a lamb. Some sources say, "In like a lion, out like a lamb." Where is the beginning of this folk wisdom, I wonder? I've even heard it called "an old Pennsylvania saw." But I see depictions of this proverb in vintage paintings. One such painting shows a graceful woman dressed in Greek clothing. She is walking in the center of the picture, with a lion striding behind her. A little lamb is pictured on the path directly in front of her. In some Christian literature, the lion and lamb are symbolic images, and the month signifies the end of winter as well as the life of Jesus. The beginning of spring signifies the resurrection into a new life. It's the transformation of Christ from His earthly life to His heavenly life. He is called the Lamb of God and the Lion of Judah.

If you live in an area of the country that experiences cold winters, you will most likely hear people grumbling about "enough snow." They say they are tired of shoveling the stuff and driving on slippery roads in snowstorms. The desire for the next season is ripe by mid–March. Spring is the topic every day, and such talk begins by mid–February each year. Don't they understand that spring won't be coming just yet? It's still wintertime! Our seasons have a rhythm, set into place by the Creator when this universe was created by His hand. Yet generations of humanity keep wishing for something different. Why?

Can we take a moment to think about why people always long for events of the future? By such future–mindedness, we will fail to take the time to appreciate the day we live in. Keep our minds on the moment we are in right now. Appreciate and embrace this one moment, whatever you are doing, and wherever you are as you read this essay. Hold on to this day, for it will never come again. You will be here for today only. Our Creator gives us grace for today. Discover the grace of the present moment and you will discover the most powerful force in this universe. Grace. Allow yourself to be absorbed in the grace of the present moment. It is the joy of life!

The only fact we know for sure is that we are *here, today*. If we constantly look forward to another time, another season, another year, another job, another spouse, another home, another activity, another life, we never experience the one day that we are living right now. Please don't wish away your life. Appreciate and hold onto the special moments of today. Will you do that?

Psalm 118:24, English Standard Version, says:

This is the day that the LORD has made; let us rejoice and be glad in it.

Learn to grasp the gift of the day you have been given. You will find the beauty and peace that is here—*today!*

I'm sharing some activities we could do to help us stay in the moment:

Take a walk outside. If it's raining, take an umbrella. If it's snowing, dress warmly and put on your snow boots. If it's sunny, then bask in the warmth. Use all your *senses*.

Think about how this day *feels*.

What do you see all around you? Look up into the sky and notice the colors, clouds, movements, direction of the wind, and even how the birds are flying above your head or how the trees are waving in the spring breeze.

Can you *hear* the sounds of traffic? Birds? Other people? Pets?

How about the sounds of your own footsteps? Your breath?

Can you feel your pulse? Your beating heart?

Try to describe what you are hearing. Be quiet while you tune your attention to the sounds.

Can you *touch* this day with your hands? Touch a tree and pay attention to how it feels. Your feet are carrying your entire body as you walk. How do they feel?

Can you inhale and exhale? How does this movement make your body feel?

Can you *smell* the air? What else do you smell when you stop to think about it?

I wrote a poem about how I experienced my own world this month. It's called "March Arrived Like a Capricious Cat." The poem you read in the beginning of the March section of this book gives insight into my own exploration of this month. I took a photo of the scene outside. The frozen wind chimes hanging from the tree branch inspired me to look closer at the whole scene. It was snowing, and the snowflakes showed up in my photos. I wanted to remember this moment because it was breathtaking. Sacred and holy.

Right now, this would be a good time to turn back to the beginning of March and read the poem again now that you have new information.

How did I share my own feelings about this month?

It's your turn to write about your own day. If you like music, why not compose a little tune or jot down some lyrics about your discoveries? This day belongs to you. Grab onto it and claim it for your own. Don't waste it by dwelling on tomorrow. Set your intentions to describe and experience this day and see what happens.

This could be a great day to take a photograph, like I did! I walked out into the winter sunshine and took some photos in the area around my Zen Meditation Garden to preserve the memory of how it looks today. In my poem and my photographs, I have captured the essence of a month that comes in like a lion and goes out like a lamb.

What does it look like where you live today?

How can you capture what you experience today?

Silver Cloud Dancers

Silver clouds swirl & spin in circles
Inflated silence above her golden head. She
Levitates above the floor reaches for
Variable visions of mesmerizing cloud–pillows.
Eternally drifting in uncertain lifecycles
Round & square. Touch the floating orbs.

Cloud dancer stretches her slender hands
Longevity is unpredictable uncertain
Out–of–the–box survival fluctuates
Undulates
Determined by chemistry & chaos.

Dance your memories in silver clouds
Air and pure helium lift in rhythm
No one can calculate your journeys
Choreography of individual flights
Every Friday morning new clouds arrive
Repeat the process of new expectations
Some silver clouds last for a week. Some less.

APRIL

Muddy Hands

*You turn things upside down! Shall the potter be regarded as
the clay, that the thing made should say of its maker, "He did
not make me"; or the thing formed say of him who formed it,
"He has no understanding"?*
—Isaiah 29:16

Breaking News! October 2007
I suddenly lost most of my eyesight.
I did not know night from day.
I could not see a clock. Time vanished.
I could not find a phone number or dial a phone
"Normal" was now upside–down days and nights.
I could dream.
I could still envision wonders.
I could try. I could try, again.
I picked up a piece of wet clay.
Slowly, the muddy substance felt like
    a new possibility in my hands.
The clay brought back memories.
My muddy hands began to do the work
    of remembering
Muddy hands gave new confidence inside of me.
Muddy hands brought wholeness.

I dug into the mud, made unexpected treasures. The wet clay gave itself to me. "Magic Spirit Treasure Boxes" emerged. Cherished objects. Wall sculptures to honor the Earth, Nature, and the healing of my broken eyes. When I use my muddy hands, I am completed.

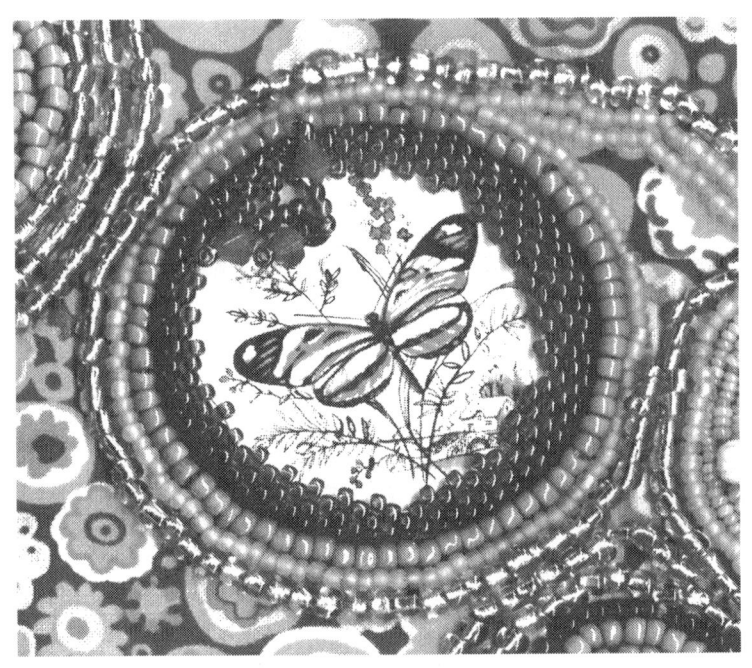

A Visitation from Butterflies

When I see a butterfly in a summer field, it brings back a specific memory. The impressions are as vivid as they were ten years ago, when I witnessed something miraculous! My rare observation was not in warm weather, nor was it outside in a field of flowers. What I witnessed took place on a frigid winter day in a large urban hospital room, in the Intensive Care Unit.

I watched quietly while two butterflies played together in the stillness of thin air, as though time had vanished. This vision I saw happened unexpectedly, just a couple of months after I lost most of my eyesight to a rare disease. I had not yet had any rehabilitation or training and could no longer see my own face in a mirror.

I lingered for hours at the bedside of our daughter, Heidi Melinda. She was in a medically induced coma following surgery to remove two cancers. After the surgery that removed ovarian and kidney cancers, it looked like she was in serious trouble. She was on life support, not breathing on her own. Her lungs were failing.

Heidi was motionless. Tubes sprouted out of her body and ran up to the ceiling or were attached to machines on both sides of her bed. Watching over Heidi, I felt like I was living in a netherworld. I seemed to be viewing my daughter through a sheer gray curtain that no one could pass through. I felt helpless.

Heidi's coma lasted for two weeks. Nurses and doctors were at her side or directly outside her transparent room as they controlled the computers connected to her room full of equipment. Someone sat at the computer continuously to watch her vital stats and medication controls. Hospital staff called her the Sleeping Princess.

I sat in a chair at the foot of her bed. My blurry eyes tried to focus on her. I realized suddenly that Heidi and I had two unexpected visitors. They had not come in through the door.

I watched in silence as two enormous butterflies emerged from the atmosphere near her feet. I saw them distinctly, in every detail and in full color. I saw them closer than I had ever seen a butterfly before that day. The brilliantly vibrant pair flew gently, gracefully forward. They appeared to be playing with each other, as butterflies do when you see them gliding and hovering around the dancing blossoms in a field on a summer day.

These two butterflies were a deep crimson red. Each graceful wing was the size of my hand. They were bright, velvety, and generously proportioned. In all my life, I never saw a butterfly as large as this mysterious pair. I watched them, and it was as though they were dancing together. Yet the frolicking butterflies were the most normal scene I could ever experience.

I knew they were not ordinary butterflies! This was a miraculous moment, something from another time and place. Heidi's body became the field over which the butterflies zig–zagged back and forth. They moved so elegantly towards her head. I watched them for what felt like a long time, but I believe it was probably only seconds. The dance of the red butterflies was like an eternal moment when time did not exist.

They gave me hope for my daughter's recovery. I sensed that they were a pictorial symbol of the Holy Spirit. I felt an inner peace and divine assurance at that moment.

Spring sunshine brings us the beginning of flower gardens that will turn into a riot of vibrant colors we will enjoy until the end of the autumn season.

Time passes, though, and in our joy of the moment, we are unaware when the days begin growing shorter. Months and years pass. We barely notice the changes. The glorious dance of the butterflies, insects, and wildflowers gradually changes. There is a final time of blazing colors when everything intensifies. Autumn, we'll recall, brought a different kind of landscape to our vision. It was a beauty more intense than our summer days had been.

Sometimes a person will mention how they suddenly saw a butterfly that appeared unexpectedly after a loved one died. They appear without warning, and often they fly around a person. One friend told me how she experienced a head–butting from a butterfly one day. It was as though the delicate insect was trying to get her attention. It seems the butterfly is trying to communicate with a human. Butterflies arrive in pairs, at times. I wonder if they are exceptionally bright and larger than life. Do they appear to be otherworldly, so that you could not possibly miss seeing them? In my experience, I knew for sure they were not of this world.

Traditionally, it is believed that butterflies are harbingers of renewal, transformation, healing. Since that day when I saw the butterflies, I began to use the motif in some of my artworks. It's an ancient symbol, with deep roots as a metaphor in folklore and the narrative accounts of antiquity. Inspiration and ideas flow or surround us as we seem to stand in an invisible, yet powerfully present, landscape.

Many writers from a variety of cultural and religious backgrounds speak of the awareness of divinity they experience when they reflect on nature.

Throughout Christian history, there is a recurring theme of recognizing the work of God when we view nature. But we find this theme long before Christianity existed in the relics and objects left behind in antiquity by pagan cultures.

This theme is expressed by one of the most memorable hymns of all, "How Great Thou Art." This example is found in the second stanza:

When through the woods and forest glades I wander
And hear the birds sing sweetly in the trees;
When I look down from lofty mountain grandeur
And hear the brook and feel the gentle breeze;
Then sings my soul, my Savior God to Thee,
"How great Thou art! How great Thou art!"
Then sings my soul, my Savior God to Thee,
"How great Thou art! How great Thou art!"
—Carl Boberg

People of all ages expressed thoughts about butterflies.

The Mandarin Chinese word for butterfly means "70 years." Therefore, in their culture, butterflies are a symbol of a long life.

Japanese tradition says the butterfly is thought to be representative of maidens and marital bliss. Many Japanese families use the butterfly image in the family crest design.

Germans' unique belief is that butterflies can often be found hovering around milk pails or butter churns. The German word for butterfly is *Schmetterling*. This is one of my favorite German words. It's actually derived from the Czech word *smetana*, meaning "cream."

In literature we find numerous references to butterflies from ancient times to the present.

Traces of butterfly imagery are deeply ingrained in Western civilization. Ancient Greeks believed a butterfly was the soul of someone who had died. Their word for butterfly is "psyche." Translated, it means "soul."

Early Greek art features images of butterflies on vases. Butterflies are featured in their mythological tales. It is a recognition of the presence of a spiritual aspect. We are more than a physical body; we possess a divine spirit that is invisible and eternal. We can read from the beginning of the Bible, in Genesis, that humans were created to live in a beautiful garden and to tend it. We were created to be friends with God; we were made to live forever with God.

We can find references to the butterfly as a soul in the lore of Russia and Ireland. There, the butterflies are always symbolic of a celebration and resurrection.

One important aspect of Christian faith is the hope of resurrection. The symbol of the butterfly is an important image to Christians. You will find this image used particularly at Easter, when we think of the life cycle of the butterfly. We get the picture that signifies how Jesus was put to death, and after three days, He arose. Every person who has accepted Jesus into his or her life is filled with the resurrection power of Christ.

At Christian funerals and memorial services, there will usually be references to a butterfly as an example of how we all will shed our body at death, and then we will come alive again with Christ. Of course, this belief is a familiar theme in almost all mythology. Resurrection is a recurring theme in many myths and cultures, as I have explained. I think all faith traditions embrace the butterfly as something very special.

Let's take a look at 1st Corinthians and we'll find a marvelous promise.

So will it be with the resurrection of the dead. The body that is sown is perishable, it is raised imperishable; it is sown in dishonor, it is raised in glory; it is sown in weakness, it is raised in power; it is sown a natural body, it is raised a spiritual body.
—1 Corinthians 15:42–44

Don't be surprised if one day you see a shimmering butterfly flying around you in an unusual way. It could be a time when you feel helpless or broken, as I did. It may happen at a time when you least expect a visitation or are thinking that nobody cares about you. Just smile!

It's been a decade since Heidi was visited by butterflies. Our Sleeping Princess remains free of ovarian and kidney cancers.

For the story behind Carl Boberg's poem, see https://en.wikipedia.org/wiki/How_Great_Thou_Art#Inspiration

Kaleidoscope:
Collecting Patterns of Light and Dreams

For behold, the winter is past, the rain is over and gone. The flowers appear on the earth, the time of singing has come, and the voice of the turtledove is heard in our land.
—Song of Solomon 2:11–12

Patti and I walked down a narrow stone path one spring afternoon in the mid–1950s. Our pastel plaid dresses fluttered slightly in the soft afternoon breeze. We removed our cotton sweaters, draped them carelessly over our arms, and held onto our folded umbrellas for the journey home. We swung our empty metal lunch pails back and forth in the air, keeping time with our steps.

Like most days during this time of changing seasons, it rained in the early morning before we left for the mile-long walk to school. A few hours later, the day took a turn in a new direction and warmed up significantly. My sister and I felt happy because the rain stopped. But now, we meandered at an easy pace in the opposite direction. School was over for the day and there was no reason to walk faster. Soon we stood beside a large field.

We both paused for a moment, tilting our heads up to smell the clean, sweet aroma rising up from the thick blanket of wood violets. The anticipation slowed us down even more as we scanned the lush, wide field. In a moment, without speaking to each other, we dropped our belongings at the edge of the path and stepped lightly between the moistened, deep-green leaves.

We were absorbed in the moment, bent over the deep-blue violet blossoms, and soon gathered some dainty flowers into a bouquet. One by one, we snapped the fragile, yellow-green stems of the violets, placing each one carefully in the grasp of a free hand. When our small hands could hold no more violets, we stepped away from the field and ambled towards our home, where our mother was awaiting our arrival.

We burst into our 1920s wood-frame house through the back door. We ran to Mom to give her the little bunch of spring flowers. She put the bouquets in water to keep them fresh and placed them on a windowsill in the kitchen.

I am a great-grandmother now, but I still live near the neighborhood where I grew up. The two-story red brick school was torn down years ago, but a much smaller portion of the once expansive farmer's field remains. Much of this delightful green space was sold off when the farmer grew too old to plow his fields any longer. A new highway replaced the two-lane country road that we walked beside on the stony pathway as children. Occasionally, I still walk on that path. It is a conduit to childhood memories.

The smallest details in a late spring landscape come alive with ever-changing patterns of light and shade.

Delicate new leaves appear to be sprinkled with transparent silvery crystals. At the edge of a meadow, I stretched my arm into the air and felt the velvet softness of sumac branches. When I glanced down towards the earth, I became aware of the deep layers of last autumn's leaves intermingled with shoots of new grass. I noticed some budding pink hyacinths growing beneath a tree.

In springtime, the whole world seems like we are looking through a kaleidoscope because we see patches of brilliant colors everywhere in our landscape.

The word "kaleidoscope" has Greek roots. It means "a form beautiful to see." I am compelled to ask you, "When is the last time you held a kaleidoscope in your hands, with one eye focused through the small, round window? Do you recall the vivid colors, the ever–changing shapes, as you slightly moved your hand around the barrel of the magical object?"

With a slight twist, all the shapes fall into new pictures. Hidden fragments inside the instrument form numerous, shifting shapes. In a moment, the view looks like a whole new world inside the kaleidoscope.

My sister and I picked violets in that field over six decades ago. At times, I can still have that feeling like I did as a little girl. I've always been enchanted with small delights I find in nature and in the changes that come with each season. The passing of time is like that, too. With just a small twist of the wrist, a slight shift in the breeze, a new thought flutters in my mind, and I am taken into an entirely new landscape. I am changed.

I wonder: Can I find my way back to the inner sense of

peacefulness and wonder that I encountered as a little girl who picked violets along a rural path?

Winter is over. A slight turn of the kaleidoscope. Birds are singing. Everything feels fresh. Spring arrives. Transformation.

Can you describe what you feel as the colors dance and flow over the mirror images inside? And did you know that inside the kaleidoscope are tiny, ordinary objects, such as buttons, stones, chips, and fragments? Every illusion you enjoy viewing is merely a collection of ordinary little things someone gathered and put inside with mirrors set at 60–degree angles.

It was more than six decades ago, when I picked wild violets with my sister in a rural farmer's field, that I began to realize I had a deep faith in a Creator. I experienced so much happiness and a strong sense of wonder at the beauty that surrounded me. Just as I remember how I felt on a spring day when I picked flowers with my little sister, I am still stopped in my tracks by the beauty of nature.

I know! It's always the big, bold, loud, dramatic events that make headline news. It is usually the glitzy events and celebrated people who are sought after for the highlights we see in the evening news.

I've noticed there is no mention of the ache we often feel in our inner being and the elusive feeling that something is just not right. Oh, I know about that yearning that whispers from deep inside my body.

Could it be that once again I have walked on that familiar pathway from my schooldays?

Or was it a different path that led me to places where I

was not called by God to be? At times we all take a wrong path. And when we do, there is always a sense of discomfort and painful stumbling blocks to be experienced when we are outside our calling. I do believe that each of us has gifts and something to do in this world that is for us alone to experience. We don't always get it right; I am certain of that. Fortunately, we can turn around, retrace our steps if we have to, and go back to where we need to be.

The question is, how to find our way back to the little path where we experienced the joy of picking spring violets? It's an inner space. It's deep inside us.

Sometimes, we find that it comes when we just sit quietly in silence, listening for God's still, small voice. Like a kaleidoscope, we find the small treasures all around us. When I sit down and spend time alone, in silence, I experience transformation. I turn another bend, there is a shift in perspective, and those little gifts are reflected by the mirrored light. I am transformed yet again by small gifts.

God works just like that!

The longer we look at Him, the more our faith grows. Each turn we take towards Him opens up a new landscape that shows us insight into His character.

I approach quietly. Slowly, I realize the rain has stopped. I tilt my head towards the sky, listening for the songs of the circling birds overhead. I listen to hear the voice of the turtledoves as they hover above the tall pine trees. It is happening again. Something new. Flowers are beginning to bloom and spring has come to Earth one more time. My feet are damp from the early morning shower. Just another small turn of the kaleidoscope—and winter is past.

Yes! I see now—transformation.

MAY

Slowly, Suddenly: Remembering Persephone

Ripe for contemplation
the sun moves slowly
to center sky
stillness.
I remember
the springtime
picking flowers
things happen suddenly.
I drift in random circles
on the surface of quiet waters
beneath clustered branches.
the day can change suddenly
no movement in the tangled leaves
even birds seek shade today.
We danced through wildflowers
suddenly
we are invisible
and grow old.
I shift forward
undulating slowly
to an old rhythm

summer's sleep returns.
Randomness brings quick changes
this evening is like
the moment before my birth
a full moon will rise this evening.

When I Begin My Day with Mozart

I put the morning coffee on to brew, reach for a CD of Mozart's Violin Sonata in B–flat, carefully placing it in the CD player in the kitchen, and push the Play button. The soft and slow opening lines of the Largo–Allegro begin as I listen. A piano and a violin are filling my kitchen with sounds from centuries ago. I close my eyes and listen awhile before I continue writing my essay. There is something about Mozart's music that makes me stop whatever I am doing; it takes me back in time. But it's not the time in the 18th century when the music was first performed for a royal audience. It is my own time at the end of the 20th century, when the music of Mozart became a core element in my own life. Thoughts of listening to this music flood my mind on the chilly November day, and those musings create layers of memories.

As the days and years come to mind, I remember Austria when it was Mozart and me.

Mozart's first performance of his original composition was April 29, 1784 in Vienna; Emperor Joseph II was in the audience. As Mozart played the piano, the emperor made a discovery. Mozart was playing from memory, for he did not have time to write the composition out on paper. The pages in front of him were blank!

My first trip to Europe in 1991 was a gift I gave myself to celebrate the completion of my MFA degree at West Virginia University. I arrived in Salzburg, Austria at the beginning of July, just in time to join in the celebration festivities for the 200th anniversary of Mozart's death. My month–long visit was filled with special art exhibitions in palaces and museums, all focused on Mozart. Mozart's life and his music surrounded me everywhere I went. I attended concerts and special exhibits during my month–long vacation. Now I was hooked on Mozart!

I came to Austria as a participant in a drawing class, and I created an entire body of work on the theme of Mozart's death and his music. I created art and wrote in a journal as I traveled.

Ten years later, my poems and reflections from that summer trip were part of a series of poems and drawings that appeared in my book *Concerti: Psalms for the Pilgrimage.*

During that first visit, I made an intention for my own life while I visited this city. I fell in love with Austria, the culture of art and music of the people I met, and the music of the masterful composers who lived in Austria over the centuries. I intended to order my life in such a way that I would spend my summers there every year. I had no idea how that would happen, or if it could happen, but I knew that would be the life I would choose to live.

Five years after my first visit to Salzburg, I accepted a tenure–track position to be a professor of fine arts and humanities at a private college in western Pennsylvania. I quickly realized there was no study program at the college that provided students with the opportunity to study in Austria or Germany. During my first year of teaching at the college, I proposed creating such a course. The following year, I was back in the city I love, with students of my own. This was the first of many years that I would have the joy of bringing students to Austria every summer, where I taught "Drawing and Writing in Salzburg."

During this course, we worked in a studio in a small village in the Alps, Monday through Thursday mornings. Most days, we met early in the morning and then traveled somewhere in the area to draw and write from the different places we explored. It was a dream that became my reality. I had the joy of sharing this magnificent country with my students every summer for a month–long sojourn. On our weekends, we traveled together to Germany, the Czech Republic, and Italy. We climbed mountains and locked our arms together as we skipped down steep mountain paths. We kept journals, wrote about cultural experiences, made drawings and paintings in the streets and along the breathtaking mountain paths. Students attended concerts and shopped and trekked through the new places we found.

Gradually, I began to realize that the seeds of what we love become the life we live when we set our intentions in that direction. I wanted to create a life where I could spend summers in Austria. I had set the dream I embraced into motion. My dream would become my life journey at a later time.

Now, sitting here in my office typing up this essay, I listen closely as the final piece of music comes to a conclusion. The piano and the violin have been playing together as I write.

The violin sonata plays on, and I listen to the rapid notes of the piano moving playfully through the house in what seems like a race with the violin. I can envision a spring afternoon and the violin and piano romping in the sunshine, chasing each other about on the lawn. At times it sounds like the piano takes the lead, yet this is not the case. The violin weaves through the many notes, and in the end they are one. I listen as applause breaks out immediately as the piano and violin strike the final note together.

This day will take me on other journeys as I walk my dogs, care for my cats, take my husband to the hospital for a checkup, and edit this essay tonight. At special moments throughout my day, I just might hear a few bars of Mozart's Violin Sonata in B–flat. I hope so!

Note: If you would like to enjoy this lovely work of art by Mozart, you can listen to it here:
https://www.youtube.com/watch?v=s–KDzAYOroI

Painting with a Needle

My mother patiently taught me how to make a variety of embroidery stitches when I was a young child, around eight years old.

One afternoon, we sat side by side in my grandmother's kitchen. Mom said, "I have a gift for you today," as she held a brown paper shopping bag. "I put together an embroidery kit for you!"

I watched closely as she reached into that bag several times and placed each item on Grandma's kitchen table. First, I saw a piece of neatly folded ivory linen fabric. Next, she held up three colors of embroidery floss. Each little package of floss had a gold and black glossy paper band around the middle, and the colorful thread seemed as bright and shimmering as that band. The shiny little skeins of thread were shades of sky blue, dark cobalt blue, and silver–gray. She handed the skeins over to me.

I held those silky skeins of cotton floss in my hands and moved them about to catch the filtered afternoon light from the window. The threads gleamed as I turned them over and over. They felt smooth and soft. The colors seemed to be magical; they were the colors of the summer sky.

Mom dipped her hand back into that bag. My new embroidery kit included a small package of slender silver needles and a round metal embroidery hoop.

As I speak of that day, I have to close my eyes for a few moments, because, I still imagine how it felt, and I envision the movements of my mother's graceful hands when she bent over me and showed me how to separate the threads, then insert the strand into the slender needle and into the soft cloth she had stretched into the metal embroidery hoop.

"Push gently down on the top of the needle. That will bring the sharp, pointy end to the back of the cloth," she said. "Now that it is in the back, we have to push it up through again, and it will be on the top of the cloth." She repeated this movement several times to show me how that will make a stitch and how the stitches will begin to look like a picture.

After I watched her make a few stitches, she handed me the embroidery hoop. I searched for just the right spot where the needle could be pushed into the cloth. I gave the needle a gentle push and it popped through to the back side. I did it again. And again. I was hooked!

I still recall a nervous feeling of excitement when I first experienced how the needle worked, gliding through the fabric, back and forth. After six decades, the recollection remains intact, alive, and vivid. Needles, cloth, threads! My lifelong love affair with the world of fabric, threads, yarn, and beads started that day.

This passion brings with it an intense desire for solitude. Fiber art is deeply personal, even sensual. Stitching is a quiet and peaceful occupation. Here is where I feel the presence of a gesture—a movement through time and space. I am always alone with my materials and my thoughts. The subtle body movements seem to have a way of setting my spirit free. Shortly after I begin working, I pass into a place where there are no limits and no boundaries. I call it timelessness. I am set free to dream.

I create talismans, amulets, and wall works in my secluded studio. I feel the magic of silken threads and the tension of moving my needles through the fabric. Each little stitch takes me further along on my life journey. I am on a pilgrimage. I make hundreds of patient stitches in the creation of just one small piece of fiber art.

That particular afternoon lesson, sitting quietly with my mother, was a gift. I often wonder: Did she recognize that I was a child destined to make exquisite, sacred objects? Somehow, she must have known intuitively that it was important to take the afternoon and spend it with her oldest daughter. Did she know that she was teaching me a life lesson with three skeins of cotton thread, a delicate needle, and a piece of ivory linen stretched inside a silver embroidery hoop?

I recognize that this embroidery lesson was my first painting lesson. Instead of a stretched canvas, we used a piece of linen stretched onto the hoop. Instead of pigments and paints, I was given colored threads. In the place of a painter's fine-bristle brush, I made my first tentative marks, my painterly strokes, with thin strands of colored threads.

I am conscious of creating a painting with a needle and beads. Gemstones and found objects become the splashes of color, my unusual pigments. But even more, I am aware of being part of a long tradition of fiber workers who developed this craft throughout the ages of human history.

Embroidery is found worldwide in museums and special antiquities collections. Several early examples are from China. They date to the Warring States period (5th–3rd century BC). I am certain we could look further back in our collective timeline to find humans who created the stitches. The fascinating thing is that from the beginnings of the early stitched fiber works, the stitches have never changed. The stitches from early examples are precisely the same as the stitches I use today in my own mixed media fiber work.

JUNE

Musings on "E"

A musical score that begins on the note of "E" is esoteric
because this third note in C Major emits
cryptic and enigmatic sounds.
Don't you see? I'd give everything to take the
Easy Pass!
Forego the electric currents of exuberant poetry—
Get down and dirty, Girls! Eliminate the end rhymes
heave away the elegance of each syllable.
I just want a poem that expels an egg or
joins every elongated line with a loud
Klink! or a curve for my envious eyes.
Link up the endangered nouns to a
myriad of enlarged verbal sounds.
No more economics of musical composition—
or exquisite conjunctions! My ears
pause between the centuries of
Quarter note rests and evocative scales
related to the ancient Greek theory of music.
Stir up the "E" sounds of the lyre and harp.

Tug them taut like elastic bands
until those elusive "E" notes
venture beyond the elemental lexicon.
Walk towards East Street where letters "E" or
"X" are symbols that elucidate something evasive.
Yank these empty letters from the English alphabet so
"Z" can represent every elemental consonant in the
   Garden of Eden.

Gestures

The professor had a euphoric smile as he paused during one of our daily breaks and gathered his students into one corner of the life drawing classroom. We all sat around him in a semicircle, our focus directed towards the man who taught us about life drawing. But it was far more than just a quick glance at the model. We were learning to look deep inside those nude bodies, to find bone structure, rising and falling muscles, the very breath of life in a human body. We learned that if we did not know how to draw the body, we would never be able to grab the essence of anything else. "The figure is a landscape," he said, "and you have to learn every nuance of the figure before you can paint anything else. Without this skill, all the rest of your art will be weak and have no structure to hold it together."

Our drawing professor leaned back in his chair, tilted his head just enough that it looked strangely slanted. His gray–blue eyes focused towards the long row of ceiling–high windows. The late morning light flowed into the spacious room. His face appeared translucent because it was illuminated by the natural light. His brown leather work boots were weather–worn and looked unevenly smooth on the bottoms. Our professor's clothing indicated that he was fond of faded jeans and T-shirts, and he seemed more like a rural coal miner or steelworker than the stuffy image people often have of a university professor. In the old room, the age-worn wooden plank floors and the professor's boots reminded me of the history of this place, where hundreds of students walked coming and going to classes.

Our teacher seemed to become a child again as he spoke about the joy of expressing life with our charcoal lines on a large page of newsprint paper. At times, he spoke directly to us, individually. It was a one-on-one commentary on what he observed on our drawing paper. He examined our smudged, jagged, smoothed or delicate drawings. He looked into our eyes as he gave his critique of what he observed. He made a joke and laughed about what he saw on the page. We laughed with him. He had a sharp wit, a critical eye; his ability to focus on a tiny bit of information was uncanny.

Spontaneous sessions, gathered around him, were special moments that we all enjoyed with him every day when we took our morning break. He affirmed our own discoveries about life and living when each of us, too, became a child again. He urged us to scribble with abandon. No restraint. For the first time in our adult lives, we realized there would never again be anyone looking over our shoulder and demanding that we "color inside the lines." This was the message of the day. It was such a simple truth that it cut deeply into my soul and took root when I eventually realized I was free to make a mess, have fun with abandon, and scribble. Yes, he talked about scribbling and having a blast when we make art. I began to splash inks and paints with enthusiasm on pages. Energetic, flying hands and intensely focused minds were okay with Professor Glen Brunken. Our acutely focused minds discovered the feeling that he proclaimed a truth that he buried inside me forever. I was free to play and enjoy the physical activity of drawing with a passion.

"Drawing is a sport." Yes, he proclaimed it! "Drawing is a sport," he continued, speaking in his clear, slow Oklahoma drawl. "You are athletes! You'd better be standing at your easel when the Muse arrives!"

I sat up straighter and pulled my shoulders back, taking in a long breath of pride in my profession. "I am an artist!"

I first encountered the paintings of Glen Brunken one afternoon when I walked slowly through a museum exhibition. I stopped suddenly when I came to a painting that was named "Little Yellow Painting." I had the feeling that I didn't need to breathe anymore; all I wanted was to just stand there forever, gazing into the deep brush strokes and thick slashes of vibrant yellow oil paint. This little gem of a painting was done on stretched canvas. I had to tear my eyes away from the surface of this brilliant ray of vivacious, powerful strokes to have a look at the tag on the gallery wall:

"Little Yellow Painting"
Acrylic on Canvas
Glen Brunken, American (1943—)

I recognized his name, and I knew he taught at a local university. In that moment, I knew this was an inspired teacher who danced with the mysteries in his paintings. I enrolled in his summer drawing class at the university. And this is how I became one of his students, sitting in the circle as he proclaimed the duties and the joy of being an artist.

During the regular semester, he offered printmaking courses, but it was his summer drawing classes where I learned what it meant to be an artist. The early morning figure–drawing classes were intense because we absorbed life lessons while developing our drawing skills. Drawing was hard work. Learning to see is a difficult journey. In our daily discussions, we expanded our core philosophy and talked about making art. Like all fine arts professors, Glen was well read in philosophy and literature. He spoke about various genres in a way that directed us to weigh out our ideas on a broad spectrum of intuition that crossed all boundaries and disciplines. Glen sharpened our minds. I became a pencil that had been rubbed on sandpaper. Sharp.

In the heat of the early morning, our summer drawing classes were intense. We were dedicated workers who stood at our easels hour after hour, day after day.

Professor Brunken once reminded me, "Making art is a profession. It's your job. You go to work every day, just as if you worked in a factory. You bring your lunch bucket to work, and you take your place at your easel."

He instilled in us a sense of pride in our profession and a strong work ethic. We had business to do, and we needed to understand that we had to focus on getting the work done. This was our life work, our calling, and our mission.

We did not have air conditioning, but the wall of open windows was adequate. A slight breeze wafted across the large room; it was enough to keep us going. Our minds focused on the lines we were putting down on the paper. We labored at our easels, drawing from the live model. We stood in a circle around the nude model's platform. The rudiments of making art soaked our consciousness. This was the battlefield where we struggled to find the forms and planes; we kept our eyes focused on the variety of models who took a pose on the model's platform. That square, foot-high, wooden platform became the center of concentration and the apex of the world that connected us to our internal longings to find balance and purpose. As our model stood tall, reached out, bent from the waist, twisted sideways, or lunged into a classical Greek warrior pose, each art student guided pieces of black charcoal sticks, worn-down or sharply ground lead pencils, blocks of waxy crayons, or even brushes and paints. In turn, we slashed, swooped, smudged, splattered, jabbed, or trickled our materials onto the intimidating sheets of drawing paper. Our daily skirmishes with thick drawing boards held upright on tall metal easels were the challenge we all faced.

After four hours of drawing, my hands, arms, face, and clothing were covered with the materials I had used for my drawings. I felt like a small child who was playing in the mud—joyous and forbidden. It seemed that for the first time in my adult life, I could get very dirty and I was breaking the rules—and it was all okay. I relished my days making drawings with my classmates, and I felt as though I was part of something so powerful, it could never be expressed in words.

Prior to entering the university to begin work on a degree in art, I had already studied painting for nearly ten years. I was passionately in love with the act of painting. My paintings appeared in national exhibitions, and I won many awards at juried shows across the country. I was a painter who was enchanted with the landscape and made paintings that are called "painterly realism." I already understood that painting was my calling in life. I read art books and studied the photographs of drawings and paintings. I visited art exhibitions and looked closely at each work that interested me. I learned from them first hand and brought information and techniques into my own art. Now I wanted to earn degrees in fine art so I could move forward into my dream job. My intention was to become a professor of fine art. There was no Plan B in my life.

At the age of forty–two, I was a nervous freshman student surrounded in the classroom by young students who were the age of my own children. In fact, I had grandchildren, too! I tried not to be self–conscious or intimidated by their youth. I stayed focused on my inner sense of purpose. I was at the university to learn everything. As I scanned the possibilities of courses available, I felt like a child who was on a merry–go–round.

Professor Brunken challenged his students. "Take courses in everything, and particularly in the things you know nothing about," he said.

Many of us began the adventure into the studies of everything with courses in geology, biology, psychology, philosophy, literature, mythology, and sociology. It all opened up a universe of new things to learn and new imagery to bring into the art we created.

He urged us forward. "Put everything you learn into your art. Every discipline offers you new information to bring back to art!" he exclaimed, as his pale blue eyes flashed quickly around the walls of the art room through the wire–rimmed glasses he kept pushing up on his face.

From that first moment when I stood in an art gallery and examined the "Little Yellow Painting," I had a secret, hidden desire as I entered that university program. My personal hidden desire was to learn to make abstract art. I saw abstract paintings in several subsequent gallery visits, and I was swept away by the magic and depth of the deeply textured surfaces. The artist's hand was visible in each work. I perceived something so mysterious and spiritual in gestural abstraction, and I began the pursuit of reading every book I could find on the artists who did this kind of painting. Their stories gave me an emotional response like nothing else. I bought several books on this way of working and did a lot of experiments on my own before I started classes. Soon my desire to make abstract art came to the forefront of my mind, and I began changing. I did abstract art in my dreams at night; during the days, I struggled to learn how to do it in the classroom.

This new world, exciting as well as frightening, forced a departure from my comfort zone, turned my focus away from previous ways of thinking and working. Professor Brunken was the catalyst that pushed me over the edge into this new consciousness and understanding of the world. Art–making at this time brought me to questions of how to work in conceptual ways. The obvious, discernible landscape of my own personal world was in flux. Our professor's views on drawing, and even his views on time and place, influenced me significantly.

For homework each day, he required us to do several pages of rapid, small drawings known as gesture drawings. Our sketchbooks filled up with pages of those little drawings—about twenty per page. As he reviewed our sketchbooks, he wrote a few messages next to gestures he particularly liked. He placed a tiny asterisk beside some of the best gestures to draw our attention to them.

Mornings in the classroom guided our understanding of the gestures of life. We made small gesture drawings as homework; in the classroom, we scribbled out large gesture drawings on our sheets of drawing paper. We learned to look into the surface of a figure, to quickly assess the gesture to see internal movements of everything. We encountered gestures at a distance. We recognized gestures in the trees, in flowers blowing in a field, a person walking far away down the busy street, the furniture in the art studio.

"Everything in our world holds a gesture. That unique gesture is the moving, living, life form of everything we are viewing. It is life, movement, and stability," he said.

Eventually, I reached the Plan A goal I had set for my own life. It was not a quick or easy path, but I became a professor of fine arts and humanities. Of course, my students learned all about gestures, as I passed down the information I had learned in my own years of studies.

One important lesson took place one day as I observed Professor Brunken as he judged an art exhibition. He looked at a sculpture and said, "This person needs to take some drawing classes. This sculpture has a lack of understanding of structure. It looks like the artist does not know how to draw."

Professor Brunken looked at a stone sculpture and knew if the artist had studied drawing and understood the gesture. In time, I learned how to identify good drawing skills, too.

Since those distant summer days as a student, I continue to observe everything in life through the lens of gesture. In my travels over the years, I always carried a sketchbook. On the pages, I jotted down quick notes or longer reflections side by side with my sketches. I recorded the gestures of the world as I experienced it. Gestures mingle among my more detailed drawings, poems, short essays, and historical notes.

Sometimes, the smallest things in our daily life begin to dance before our eyes when we look more closely at any movement. The spirit of the object is right there. The embrace of the inner core of all of existence presents itself to us. A gesture sends a powerful signal that can be discovered through all our senses. While we engage in the various movements and acts of life, every moment of every day, we are typically unaware of the message that an onlooker is getting by watching us.

Many of our actions are basically non-social, having to do with problems of personal body care, body comfort and body transportation; we clean and groom ourselves with a variety of scratchings, rubbings and wipings; we cough, yawn and stretch our limbs; we eat and drink; we prop ourselves up in restful postures, folding our arms and crossing our legs; we sit, stand, squat and recline, in a whole range of different positions; we crawl, walk and run in varying gaits and styles. But although we do these things for our own benefit, we are not always unaccompanied when we do them. Our companions learn a great deal about us from these "personal" actions—not merely that we are scratching because we itch or that we are running because we are late, but also, from the way we do them, what kind of personalities we possess and what mood we are in at the time.
—From *Manwatching*, a book by Desmond Morris

Learning to find and appreciate the sparkle of life can be difficult. We are so accustomed to taking a quick glance at everything and only seeing the surface of everything. Seeing requires more time. Seeing is a skill that has to be practiced and learned, and it takes a lot of deliberate time to do it. Think of all the many images your eyes view every day as they rapidly flash before you. There are so many that you cannot even see them, because seeing comes slowly and it comes in layers. Seeing requires intention.

One day, after Professor Brunken looked through a

group of gestures in my sketchbook, he turned to look at me and said, "Lynda, you need to look at this gesture drawing until you begin to realize it is beautiful. In fact, cut this one out of your sketchbook and put it in a frame. Put it in a place where you can see it. Look at it often. Keep looking at it until you understand that it is beautiful."

The central theme of everything is the gesture at the core of it all. I think of "gesture" as the recognition of God when He leaned down over His new creations and breathed the breath of life, His own Spirit, into them. Some days, I focus on looking more closely at the people I am in contact with, and I whisper to myself, "Look for what is good in her. Keep your focus on the inner core, on her gesture. Look again. She is made in the image of God. Take a long, slow look and find her eternal gesture. See it."

****

Note

In memory of Professor Glen Brunken (1943–2013).
Glen taught at Slippery Rock University of Pennsylvania for 40 years (1969—2009).

Two Friends on a Bench

I walked on the shady, tree-lined sidewalk that meanders along the banks of the Salzach River in Salzburg, Austria one summer afternoon. An older couple sat quietly on the well-worn wooden bench. They faced the river. They were so engaged in being together, in their own private conversation, that they paid no attention to anyone else. I had the feeling they were old friends. I was intrigued by the peacefulness of these two people. I sat down in the grass so I could watch them awhile from a distance. I reached into my backpack, took out my sketchbook and pencil, and drew a little sketch of them that afternoon. The two friends sit forever in the sunshine through the passage of time, in my memory of a lazy, hazy summer day.

Two Friends on a Bench

Two friends on a bench
comfort each other
relaxed conversation
A scratch of the head
A nod, touch of the arm
A gesture of the hand, a look
the afternoon passes
two pigeons fly
under the bench
old friends never notice
the people walking by
they only see each other
from a hidden tree branch
a bird begins to sing
a love song to them.

JULY

When I Draw

I begin to draw once again. I draw for my life. I draw to create a memory to stay with me when long winter days try to make me forget summer....

Journal entry by Lynda McKinney Lambert, July 8, 1999. Salzburg, Austria.

A Summer Story

I am very small
In a summer storm
cradled on my father's lap
moving back and forth
rocking in a chair
lightning flashes
rain glazes my view
I am filled with fearful thoughts.
"Do not be afraid," he says
I ask, "Can we take the new refrigerator
with us when we die?"
"No!" he replied
"We can take nothing with us
but our love."
I saw him once again
after his death,
he was holding
my granddaughter in his lap.

Great-Grandmother Speaks

Distant, nearly forgotten summer days in her rural village moved about silently in the thoughts of Great-Grandmother today. Generations of her ancestors walked the familiar paths through the woods that surrounded her home. Branches hung low with layers of delicate, fragrant flowers, a scent that was a mixture of wildflowers. This summer afternoon was so warm that she found it hard to breathe. Rainwater dripped on her head and bare arms from the long, overhanging branches. She shook off the wetness as she watched her two dogs run ahead. This particular day reminded her of another vignette that seemed so much like today.

Her solitary walk across the wooded ridge that overlooked the winding creek below gave her time to think of the sensitive little girl she always was. She was at home in the natural world of trees and flowers. Birds seemed to call to her in every season; they flew over the meadow grasses and floated across the brilliant cerulean–blue sky. She still listened for the crows that usually called out when they passed overhead. She loved the crows best of all.

The old woman recalled childhood days and how she loved to be outdoors in all seasons. When she was very young, summertime was particularly pleasant, because she did not have to wear shoes. When summer rains began, she splashed through the falling water as it saturated her clothing and made her long hair slick and heavy. It clung to her wet shoulders. She stomped down with her bare feet because the water splashed up onto her shorts and trickled down her sun–browned legs. Her toes dug into the puddles of cool, squishy rainwater in the yard. She moved them around to explore the wet ground, and it felt so good when she slid both of her bare feet through the thick, wet, dark mud. It oozed up through her toes and covered her bare feet.

She thought of autumn, when her family gathered up the black walnuts that dropped out of the tree and spread all over the grassy lawn. They were large, leathery, yellow–green spheres, and the black walnuts were snug and tight inside the green balls. The children helped to get those walnuts out by rolling them between two bricks to break off that outer shell. They had the most unusual earthy smell, and everyone got greenish–brown stains on their hands. There were other kinds of tree nuts dropping from the trees in the woods and along the country roads. She enjoyed gathering them, and her mother saved them until wintertime, when they were eaten on winter evenings or broken up and put into pies and cookies.

These memories brought to Great–Grandmother's mind other delights that fascinated her in the back yard, the home of an assortment of chickens. Her father had built a rustic wooden chicken coop that stood just behind the gardens. Some days, she went inside the painted wooden building where the chickens laid eggs in nests built into the walls. The hens clucked and twittered softly as she reached under them. They felt so warm and soft, and her hand searched carefully for the freshly laid egg beneath each one. The hens provided a nice breakfast for the children.

Other days, she climbed up onto the roof of that whitewashed coop to watch the dusty-gray chickens scratching about on the ground as they searched for bugs. It was a safe place to sit so that the old rooster, Mr. Cocky-Lockey, could not find her. Cocky-Lockey first came to her home when he was just a fluffy little yellow chick. He was an Easter gift. But as he grew older, his sweet nature began to turn mean and he became a terror to any person who dared to be in his back yard. Cocky-Lockey had long, elegant feathers that were brilliant hues of shimmering, effervescent colors. When the sunshine was on this magnificent bird, he seemed to glow with neon flashes of light. His tail feathers looked like a waterfall of vibrant colors. His beauty belied his true personality. He was vicious and would attack with no warning. He flew up onto his victim's head so fast he was like a bolt of lightning as he landed hard with his claws outstretched. He tried to tear at the flesh of any poor, unsuspecting person who had the misfortune of coming into his territory. His razor-sharp spurs were lethal weapons as he patrolled the yard, just waiting for his next victim. Everyone in the neighborhood knew to be on the lookout for this bird. We did not need a guard dog, for we had Mr. Cocky-Lockey.

Great-Grandmother stopped for a moment to watch the dogs sniffing along the side of the damp trail. She sucked in her breath for a moment and seemed to savor a new memory. She thought of her favorite childhood foods. They were all gathered by her father. He carried home an assortment of freshly picked mushrooms he had collected in the woods. He knew precisely where each kind of mushroom grew and exactly when each would be ready for picking. Like all woodsman in a rural area, he knew the ways of the woods and brought its bounty home for his family of four children. There was always plenty to eat because of her father's skills in hunting and gathering.

Great-Grandmother was the oldest child in the family. She might be found in the gardens, where she made deep trails and gravel roads through the dark, rich soil. She liked to play in the dirt with her dump trucks and brightly painted metal cars. She was an unusual, solitary child who did not play with baby dolls or have tea parties with her friends. She read about dainty girls who liked those things in the books she brought home from the library. She enjoyed reading about the tea parties and the adventures of young children in the books. But that was not really her world. It was the earth that she connected with. The earth in all its many manifestations became her muse from the earliest days of her life.

Great-Grandmother told me one day, "I guess I am getting old, because I am now in my 70s."

Even though she was growing older, it was apparent

that she still loved the feeling of the earth beneath her bare feet. She liked to feel it in her hands. She often sat on the ground with her strong, slender legs spread out, as though she wanted to cover as much ground as possible with her lithe body. She encouraged us to lie on the earth under the majestic pine trees in the shade. We children often reclined on the earth with her, and we all laughed, told stories, and dreamed together. It felt so good to lie there as she looked up through the sky holes in the tree above. We lay there, flat on our backs, pasted down onto the surface of the earth as though it were a magnet. Together, we gazed into the canopy above us, and beyond into the heavens.

She spoke gently as she told us, "Our bodies need the earth. We were created to be one with the earth. Remember, the first people were made from earth. The Creator has a special love for the earth and He has an everlasting love for the people He made, too. The earth helps us remember where we came from."

My body felt so heavy when I was flat on the soft, pine-covered hillside. She spoke again and said, "The earth is a positive charge and people are a negative charge. It is necessary for us to join our body with the earth's surface to become complete. We are just like a set of magnets. The positive and the negative charge have to be together for the magnet to work properly."

Our unconventional great-grandmother spoke to us one afternoon about a day she had thought about from the time when she was a very young girl. She reflected on it for a little bit of time, and I noticed she seemed like she was far away from us. Her eyes were the color you only see when you look deep into the bottom of the creek, when the sun shines down on the surface of the flowing waters. Sometimes, her haunting eyes looked golden yellow in the afternoon light as we lay under the pines on this little hillside outside her cabin.

After some time, she laughed out loud for a few seconds and then began to tell us a story.

"I believe it was probably near the middle of summer, because the days were smoldering and languid. The bright sun was high in the sky very early in the morning that particular summer. The grass was discolored, like the tan straw that snapped as I walked on it. There were some leaves, all shriveled and curled up, there on the grass, too. I heard the sound in the hot afternoon breeze. It was a symphony of insects, all singing together like a high–pitched chorus. Was it the locusts? I really can't recall exactly where the sound came from, but it seemed to me that the sounds were coming from the sky and the trees— even from the grass. I walked in my bare feet across that dry, golden grass, and I could smell a slightly musty scent in the air that day."

Great–Grandmother paused for a time and took a deep breath. I thought she was trying to bring as much air into her lungs as she could. Her entire body seemed to heave, to take in the afternoon air. She inhaled through her nose. *She held her breath for a long time*, I thought. I heard her begin to release her breath, and she exhaled through her open mouth. I watched as she did this many times. She relaxed more and more. I could almost feel how she was settling down as I watched her and listened to the quiet sounds of her breath and the radiating sounds of the insects that seemed to surround us. This day was so peaceful.

She continued her story.

"The days were so intense and hot that my skin felt sticky all the time. My hands seemed like they were dipped in wet glue, and I kept trying to separate my fingers. My long, sun-washed hair felt wet from sweating when I played in the trees that summer afternoon. I kept thinking about how my body felt so hot and dirty, and I was aware of the stifling heat of the early afternoon. I am sure I must have looked so very small to anyone who observed me as I stood beneath the large, leather-textured tree. I was a small girl, but I was bold and strong. Neighbors called me 'a wild child.' I suppose that was because my feet were always bare and I ran across the hot gravel in the driveways and the sizzling pavement. My feet were thick on the bottoms, so I really didn't feel the stones or the heat that much!

"I glanced up into the gnarled branches, with their downward movement towards the earth. The apple tree had a central trunk, and just about three feet from the ground, it had split itself somehow into three parts. I can still remember how I felt the pinch on my bare feet and how it felt to wedge each foot, carefully, into the low separation to begin the climb upwards into the tree.

"The old tree always felt like it had strong, throbbing muscles, and the skin of it was crackled on the branches that reached out in every direction over my head. The tree trunk and branches felt cool and rough. It was so shady under the tree, and I liked it because I felt like I was all alone in the entire world. Shimmering dapples of sunlight filtered through the thick leaves, and the little spots of light danced on the ground all around me. It made me think I might be dancing on a stage. I was all alone on that stage, like a ballerina. I was always a star. The shimmering lights streamed down all around me and all over my body. Some days, I danced in circles below the shady tree."

Great–Grandmother smiled, and her eyes were closed as she seemed to be watching herself dancing. Again, there was a silence, and shortly, she began to speak of how she felt when she danced in the beams of sunlight as a little girl.

"At first, I spiraled in a tight circle. My feet went faster and faster as I continued twirling about on the grass beneath the tree. I felt the breeze pulsing on my outstretched arms. My arms seemed like airplane propellers, moving round and round. We dipped up and down, and my arms seemed to be taking me far away into the sky. My hands vibrated and tingled, and I opened them wide as they led me off into the obscure distance, in my imagination. I thought, *I will fly like a bird! If I fly long enough, my arms will turn into wings and I will be a shiny, black crow! I will travel between the two worlds, bringing messages back and forth from the underworld.* My slender fingers spread wide apart, as the forces of the wind made them feel fat and tight. The light and I were old friends, and we spun together in ever–widening circles, around and about, under the tree, until we could barely breathe."

I always knew this hulking, giant tree was her favorite apple tree. She told me it was a protective, sheltering hideaway. I knew this ancient apple tree stood just behind our neighbor's gray, concrete-block garage. As Great-Grandmother recalled, "It was the only tree that stood in my neighbor's yard. I could not say that there were no other trees, but it is this giant one that I can still remember so clearly. It must have been very old, and looking back on the scene through the lens of my memory, it seemed to me it stood as a sentinel that separated the garage from the rows of garden plants."

I can tell you for sure, Great-Grandmother knew for a certainty that this tree separated and divided the back yard, but it also connected Heaven and Earth. In her childhood adventures, it was the space between here and there—between the present moment and the future. The tree stood as a vertical division in a horizontal, verdant landscape—an axis mundi. For Great-Grandmother, this tree was magical.

My great-grandmother knew then, just as surely as she knows now, about secret things. She is familiar with hidden places and what they signify. This wise woman discerned the life inside rocks and the tears that are inside the rocks. She had the gift of imagination. Silent and quiet things are most often unnoticed by people who can never visualize them.

Some people call my great-grandmother a "seer." But she really cannot see very well because she said she has sight loss. Occasionally, our great-grandmother talked to us about seeing with her inner eyes. She calls this her "intuition." She says, "I see special places that people with good eyesight have never understood. Those people who take a quick look don't see all that is really there. They never learned that looking and seeing are different things. Seeing takes a very long time to do. When you remember to trust your inner feelings, then you will see very well, my dear children."

The secret places are all tucked away in our great–grandmother's memories. One by one, over the years, she shared them with her children and her grandchildren. Even now, today, she shares these memories with me, her great–granddaughter. Great–Grandmother continues to be the storyteller for our family. Just like the griot in an African village, Great–Grandmother is the one who preserves the clandestine memories for our family. She continues telling the stories that give her descendants the information we need on our own personal journey through life. I am satisfied, because she will continue to hold the ancient recollections of our ancestors in her own soul until the time is right.

Notes from the Baroque Museum

Journal entry, July 21, 1999

The text on a white label on the gallery wall reads:
"Antonio Pellegrini (Italian, 1675–1741)."

This painting is a square format with its corners painted brown. The brushwork leaves an undulating cross shape in the center where the action of the painting takes place.

A rather narrow gold frame surrounds the canvas, with the inside edges fluted like gentle waves. The nervous waves move all around the picture's edges.

Suddenly, two furious white horses criss–cross in mid air! They have no wings! One flies over and behind the other. I watch, horrified, as two other horses, one tan and one brown, fall toward the bottom left corner.

Oh, no! It is only now I realize the four horses were pulling a chariot. There has been an accident!

The chariot is overturned and the charioteer falls toward the bottom right corner. His bent leg indicates he will not fall freely through the dangerous sky; his body will be stopped as he is caught, forever, to hang upside down from the chariot.

An odd–looking being with wings hovers above the chaos—like a large gray goose. On the back of the goose–being rides a white–bearded man. He holds his right arm high above his head like a Roman orator who demands to speak. He leans toward the chariot wreck. The actions all take place in the heavens amid pink and tan clouds. The billowing clouds float upwards in a diagonal slant from the bottom left of the picture to the top right. The sky is a heavy cobalt blue, and it propels the painful white horses forward towards me. I feel the silent scream.

There seems to be a fire in the sky that sears the mane of the brown horse as he falls toward me, and I stand here watching the sky on fire and the events that are taking place before me, in the picture–framed stage.

I am helpless….

AUGUST

Along the Road

Not all days in August
are sunny and warm.
There are those days
too dismal
even for photos.
Lonely days
that come with old age,
dark days
driving alone
when old memories
mingle among
the Queen Ann's Lace
and blue Chicory
blooming along the road.

Girl on a Bench Sees Visions of Butterflies

I encounter the little girl on a warm afternoon near the end of August. I see the chestnut–haired girl as she sits on a bench outside in the sunshine. She quietly watches me. Her deep green eyes remind me of the colors I've observed when I am in a canoe floating along on the surface of a local river. When you look beneath the surface of the water, you'll see what I mean. I call this mysterious color "bottom–of–the–creek green."

The young child sits alone on a rustic wooden bench looking straight ahead. From this solitary spot, she peers out over her world and into the future, where I stand watching her today.

Her dress is a familiar blue–and–white cotton plaid with a wide, crisp, white linen collar that lies over her slender shoulders. The dress looks fresh, starched, ironed. She is pristine, like a vintage porcelain doll.

Someone takes very good care of this little girl; somebody fusses over her and cares about how she looks. She is loved, I think.

She patiently waits in her back yard for the arrival of her cousins. The cousins will come to celebrate her eighth birthday. It is 1950.

I pause and then move slowly as I walk a bit closer to her. I take just a couple of steps forward; she watches me carefully as she smiles.

"You look so happy," I whisper under my breath. Soon, I realize she is sitting under the old, deeply textured branches of a black walnut tree.

That tree is the centerpiece of her back yard, I recall.

Besides the tree, the little girl is surrounded by a field of late-summer wildflowers in full bloom. I can see the delicate Queen Anne's lace and gentle butterflies mingling among those ivory, lace-like blossoms. The scene I observe is motionless, because this picture is frozen in a moment of time by a Brownie box camera. The photographer for this special day is her mother.

The vintage photo of the little girl is faded into shades of gray. Once it was a sharp-focused photo in glossy black and white. The child and her world feel like a dream as I continue to look. The photo was laminated long ago to the back of a small, round, glass pocket mirror. Her proud mother once carried the mirror in her handbag. In her old age, her mother gave the mirror to the little girl, who is now a grandmother. Even though the mirror was cracked in half at some time in the past, it was still a beautiful photograph in near-perfect condition.

I am an artist, and I chose this particular photograph for the central image of the art work that I have named "Girl on a Bench Sees Visions of Butterflies." It hangs here on the art gallery wall today as I walk towards the artwork.

"Girl on a Bench Sees Visions of Butterflies" is quite a

small work that represents a personal and private memory. The mixed-media fiber art measures approximately twelve inches square. A viewer must come close to it in order to see this child sitting in her backyard garden of summer dreams and childhood delights.

The images on this fiber art piece are hand-worked over the top of the 1940s vintage fabric; the picture was created from a black-and-white fabric with sharp, crisp white flowers and butterflies dancing across the surface. All this activity is on a solid black background.

There is a surprise burst of brilliant color on the black-and-white scene, though. Over the entire surface, the artist added brilliant red leaves and roses that are carved from actual coral gemstones. I feel like bouquets of red coral roses are waiting to be gathered as I look at this picture. The reality is different from that feeling because the red roses will bloom here on this picture indefinitely. Regardless of the passing seasons, this pictorial world is suspended forever outside of time.

The old-fashioned roses seem to circle around the picture, intertwining with the photo of the girl on the bench. The circular mirror image is also surrounded by layers of delicate, glistening Japanese seed beads. The glass beads are so small! They capture the light from all directions. This scattering of light from multiple sources makes the little girl in the photo seem to shimmer in her round space at the center of the picture. Visitors stop to look at the little girl in her iconic world, and they say, "It seems like we have entered into a dream world or an intimate, private vision."

Throughout this particular picture on the gallery wall, there are myriad other flower shapes made from mother of pearl and natural gemstones. In this small space we can see visions of earth and sky as we enter into this moment of time when the little girl sat patiently waiting for her birthday party to begin.

I am the blind artist who, meticulously, worked out the details of this picture. The creation of this piece was just like the process I learned to use after I lost my sight, over a decade ago. The creative work is done layer upon layer. This is how we all learn to live our lives, no matter our circumstances.

I created my self–portrait in honor of the little girl in the photo, who is me. I remembered a moment using my hands, needles, and threads to bring the viewer into the world I lived in as a child.

My slender steel needles become my paint brushes. Multifaceted beads, found objects, and natural gemstones are my "paints." Even though my physical eyes have changed my view of the world around me, my hands are quite capable of creating unique new views from my inner vision. I am still the girl on a bench, and I still see visions of butterflies in my imagination.

The Poetry Ladies

Writing is a solitary activity. It's not a spectator sport with an audience cheering you on to the finish line. A writer sets her own goals and then plans out how she will achieve the outcome she desires. We manage our own projects and we have to be self–motivators. There is nobody standing over our shoulder to cheer us on. We have to have self–discipline and plan out our days to accomplish our projects. Writers work alone in an office or dedicated writing space. Some writers like to work quietly, while others prefer to listen to music or even work outside with the sounds of nature all around them. I know of other writers who venture out with their laptops to do their writing in public spaces, such as a local coffee shop or library. Realistically, I have to say the writing life can often be lonely.

I enjoy reading stories about the famous writers who worked in faraway places such as Munich, Venice, Prague, or Paris. For a number of years, I spent summers in Europe, where I wrote and created art every day. It's inspiring to travel and keep a journal, because those writings can keep the memories fresh in our minds long after the trip has ended. My notes, reflections, and commentaries in my journals are a treasury I can go to. Those hand–written travel notes have provided me with many ideas for poems and stories over the years.

But it's not necessary to be in exotic places to be inspired. The ordinary and mundane activities of our daily life are also full of splendid possibilities for our work. Just take a look around and think of everything you can see. It is all worthy of your scrutiny and ripe to be picked for a new story or poem. We can bloom right where we are today.

Since my retirement from teaching, I work in a quiet room in my house most days. I need solitude in order to hear my inner thoughts. The only companionship I have in my writing space is my cats and dogs. They take naps in their furry beds or meander in and out during the long days of writing and editing. It's a peaceful occupation, writing. The dogs also remind me to take breaks periodically so they can go out for a little walk. It's refreshing and keeps me balanced.

In the mid–1980s, I began meeting with three local women who loved to write. We developed a deep friendship that continued for eighteen years. We met together one afternoon a month, celebrated each other's birthdays, and shared our latest writing projects. We referred to ourselves as the Poetry Ladies. I remember each woman and the projects they worked on during our writing life together. Most of our writing was poems and memoirs.

The Poetry Ladies shared some common goals. At the

top of our list of intentions was the desire to leave some of our history and our thoughts behind for our families when we were no longer with them. I think that is a priority of many writers; we desire to leave others with some memories of the times we shared with each other.

Like most writers, we each used a journal as a place to work out our ideas. At a later time, we could return to those thoughts and transform them into a poem, short story, or memoir.

Our colorful literary quartet consisted of a former newspaper journalist, the poet laureate of her county, a local newspaper writer, and a college professor. Writing was an integral part of our shared lives. We were wives, mothers, grandmothers, artists, and writers.

Our little literary group eventually ended due to life changes; we all aged. Since the three other ladies were about two decades older than me, during the later years together, everything began to change when two of the Poetry Ladies passed away and one became chronically ill. Our eighteen–year journey faded into a good memory.

When I consider the many activities we shared together, I am especially pleased about one particular project we completed as a group. We selected several poems from each of us and had them printed into a chapbook. One of the ladies was an excellent photographer, and we featured her black–and–white photos on the cover and on some pages in the chapbook. The book is a treasure for me. Just recently I sat down and read each poem by the members of our Poetry Ladies group.

My teaching career kept me occupied after the Poetry Ladies group was no longer a part of my life. As a professor of fine arts and humanities, I wrote lectures for courses and presented my papers at conferences. I taught an annual travel/study course in Europe that provided material that I developed into my book *Concerti: Psalms for the Pilgrimage*, published by Kota Press in 2002. The Poetry Ladies read most of my writings, and their input into the production of the book was invaluable. One of the special aspects of my life was the years I had with the other three ladies. There will always be a part of them in my own life.

SEPTEMBER

Adornment—September Daydreams

Adornment: Decorations worn to attract attention.

On languid September days
I would like to wear
colorful, gaudy jewelry—
every single one
at the same time.
Adornments are worn to enhance autumn days.
I'd put the gems on in layers,
I am an ancient warrior preparing for battle.
Blue topaz rings, one on each finger.
My arms, encircled with ornaments.
Protected by brilliant stones—
faceted cherry quartz, deep green turquoise chunks,
nuggets of Baltic amber in different colors,
jet–black polished stones, and waxy yellow opals.
I'll wear a periwinkle blue dancing skirt,
a flowing chiffon jacket.
I am a flamboyant coat of armor

that covers voluptuous, full breasts
like a bishop's gold–encrusted shawl.
My holy, rare, mother–of–pearl talisman
adorns my royal goddess chest.
I slip my perfumed feet into soft sky–blue sandals,
promenade around the spacious room,
in ever–widening circles,
among the evening shadows,
under luminescent spheres
turning high above us.

White Snakeroot in Bloom
Lynda McKinney Lambert, 2016

Try To Capture September

I've spent days thinking about September. How can I write a poem about her? Rapid changes are occurring all around me this month, and I'm getting dizzy! I'm downright giddy with bursts of nervous energy. This zest charge was unexpected, hidden in the mists of the crisp early morning. I floated, it seemed, at the crest of September with my feet stretched downwards to dig into the sands of its shoreline. I have been unsuccessful!

Since the beginning of this fast–moving month, I tried to pay attention to the small nuances and living details I experienced. I moved carefully, even cautiously, from day to day through the month of ever–changing September. Yes! I am standing at the midpoint of the month, and I still feel like I am lost at sea.

I take a deep breath, hold it in for a couple of seconds as I remember my fingers. I look at the computer screen. I exhale. Nearby, my sleeping dog shifts in his black, furry bed. In his sleep, he snorts, and my leather chair squeaks as my fingers pound out some letters on the stiff keyboard. I move my body forward again and bring my mind back to September. The sun streams through the dusty window.

My back seeks the stability of my solid chair. I raise my hands to my face, close my eyes, and think about my breath. As my chest rises, I become aware of the sharp, piercing call of the eagle flying above the trees outside the window.

At the beginning of the month, I took short walks in the woods. I saw subtle changes. My two dogs stopped and sniffed the breeze. They tried to catch the news of the day, to bring it home and share it with me. We paused on the path, and I watched them stop and stare into the privet bush, then up into the trees. They paid close attention to all the wildflowers as I touched them. I tried to concentrate on the details—to memorize each little fine distinction of a fragile yellow crownbeard flower or the dark blue–green leaves of the white snakeroot plant. I asked, "How does it look in the shade? How does it feel to the touch? Try to remember it all!"

I reached out, touched the trunks of trees as we traveled together in the afternoon sun. I recall the feeling of textures and the girth of a tree in my arms as I tried to encircle it. I needed to touch the overlapping surface of the locust tree, to put it in my memory bank, where I can retrieve it when wintry days become anxious and lonely.

Eventually, I realize what I searched for in September. Every new day in this quest twists and turns in on me as I search for the form that would be perfect for my September poem. I begin to visualize myself as a whirling dervish. I swirl in circles, round and round, and my feet are on sifting and shifting sand all the time. My thoughts race far faster than I could ever write. My entire body quivers inside because of all the raw sensations that this month gives me.

I realize September is the one month of the year that is a charade. She is undependable, captivating, and quixotic. She cannot be captured in the pantoum I had intended to put her into. I think, *I'll catch her by a sliver of one of her yellow petals! Then, I'll flatten her out between the pages of a villanelle.* But as it turns out, she becomes a book of sand, and I simply cannot get a grasp on her!

This morning, I tried to put some words to my paper. I had to step over obstacles of images and feelings. I said, "I have to just go after a little piece of September. I need to catch her unawares, and grab what I can. It might be just a fragment, or an adjective. Do it quickly, and run fast, bring that piece to my paper and slap it down with glue. I'll have to use E–600 for this job! What will be large enough to hold uncooperative September?

"Yes! I've got it now. My tribute to September will be an ode. It will celebrate precocious September perfectly."

My "Ode for September" must be hefty and as unsettled as she.

My ten–line stanzas will be a passionate song about September, the whirling dervish.

The Connie

The beginning of September signifies the end of summer, when nights become cooler and I begin to forget the predictable, unrelenting, steamy days and nights of July and August. Temperature readings begin to drop down into the 50s. I open the windows and feel the cool breeze move through the familiar old house. The oppressive heat and humidity of a Pennsylvania summer are swept away by the September breeze.

I sense the shift of a quickly approaching new season that is beginning to stir my senses. There is something in the air that I feel. Is it a kind of nervousness and anticipation of—what? I cannot really say.

Last night, I lay in my bed listening to the soothing insect sounds drifting upwards to my open window. The unseen creatures sounded like musicians tuning their instruments to play night songs. The sounds blended into a nocturnal symphony, a cacophony of an end–of–summer serenade.

Our century–old home is on a ridge overlooking a winding creek that meanders for fifty miles in western Pennsylvania. This long creek remains the central image of our memories throughout our lives. People from this area call it "the Connie." Its actual name is Connoquenessing Creek. For many of the residents of this village, our ancestors date back to the mid–1700s. That is when the early settlers were going back to Germany to recruit artisans to come to America and settle here. People who had skills that were needed by the colonies were recruited for about 100 years. Some descendents of the original immigrant families who settled along this creek married Indians who lived in this area.

In the summertime, the Connie comes alive with the voices and sounds of the local "crick" culture. Kayaking begins in earnest in late winter, as soon as the ice begins to dissipate. Hearty enthusiasts will continue to ride the rapids through the summer days and into the fall season. The Connie's whitewater rapids provide the perfect setting for a swift course for kayakers to perfect their skills.

On August nights, I can hear people laughing from down below the ridge. Summer nights, some people arrive here at the crick in the late evening, in the twilight, just before it gets dark. They leave their cars and trucks in a clearing beside the road, just under the old trees. Generations of local people come to spend the night fishing. I often watch as they pull out their gear. They bring coolers and jugs, flashlights, buckets of worms, fishing poles, nets, and blankets. Some of them wear baseball caps or slouchy fishing hats. One by one, they scramble down the steep, rocky path that leads to the deep water below. When they get to the bottom of the hill, they walk out onto the big, flat rock where they spend the night. I hear them talking and laughing; their voices blend in with the insect serenade.

In childhood memories, my father and I are in the backyard behind our home in the foothills. I still live in the valley between the steep hills. Like most of the steelworkers in our village, my father loved to go fishing in the Connie. In the darkness of an August night, I helped him find earthworms. His steelworker's helmet had a strange yellow light on the front of it. I smelled the acrid smoke, heard it sizzle and sputter as we bent over the dark ground. We poured mustard water down into the little tunnels where the earthworms lived. In just a few seconds, a worm came to the surface seeking fresh air, and we grabbed that worm, then sloshed it around quickly in a bowl of water to wash off the mustard water. Finally, we put the captured worm into Dad's metal pail with the holes in the sides. He had put dirt into the pail before we went searching for the worms. We turned over rocks and found creepy creatures hiding under them. Dad called them hellgrammites, and they made me shiver when I looked at them.

My favorite sight in August is the Queen Anne's lace mingled with the periwinkle blue flowers of chicory. The two wildflowers grow together along all the roads in early August. I take my camera outside so I can capture the beauty of these disorderly flowers. I imagine these fields of uncultivated flowers long after they disappear in mid–September. A friend once told me, "When you see the chicory blooming, you know winter is not far away."

Oh, I should let you know: Queen Anne's lace is my favorite wildflower because of the delicate, tiny flowers clustered on thin, celadon–green stems. The flowers seem to float in space and ride the soft wafts of the August breeze. Fragile, lacy blossoms dance in the fragrant afternoon air.

The white blossoms of Queen Anne's lace contrast with the sturdier chicory flowers. Chicory resembles a daisy, with petals branching outward from a round, dark center. Each chicory bloom has little oval petals that come to a tip that looks like someone snipped it off flat with zigzag pinking shears. The brilliant blue color of the chicory seems to pop out from among the white Queen Anne's lace in full bloom side by side with the chicory. When I see the chicory begin to bloom, I know that the season will soon be changing to autumn.

And, it always seems that it won't be long before I'll be strolling through the colored leaves on my leisurely walks through the woods along the Connie. My thoughts drift to the stories my father told me about his ancestors. I stop and look around through the woods and down to the whitewater creek. Some days, my spirit calls out to them as I look around in the world that they lived in, too. Often, I feel like I am walking over layers and generations of my family members. I ask myself, "Am I an overlay from past generations of people who lived in this place?" I recognize my ancestors' presence because they seem to surround me. I can feel them. I ask my grandmothers, "Did your feet walk on this path beside the Connie, too?"

OCTOBER

Star Signs (A Libra–Sort–of–Day)

Anyone can find the
breath of life when
creative moments
define a new morning.
Emotions & cozy
feelings are
generated by a
hearty mug of something hot.
I like to take my time
just drink my coffee nice and slow
knowing there's no rush because
limitations can't bind me.
Moments like this are timeless.
Nothing stands in my way
on autumnal days when my
poetry doesn't always rhyme.
Questions can be explored as I
re-arrange the lines I make up.
Strategies are endless
tapping out stories without a pen
Using star signs to map out new terrain.

Various writers often ask,
"What can bring a poem to life?" I reply,
Xerox copies to share a poem with friends.
Yellow paper with dark blue ink.
Zodiac notes on a Libra-sort-of-day.

Message from the Stars

Something is here, be it a message from the stars or from the booming labyrinth of the mind...or from both. It must have left a signature somewhere, a thread in the snow, the scratch of a strange nail upon a wall. And, we can certainly find that thread.... In taking the thread we might find ourselves in possession of a very real key to the universe.

Once the thread is in hand, our own mythology will tell us where it leads, for it will be the same thread that the maiden Ariadne handed to Theseus when he stood before the maze of the Minotaur.... And we will all go down the labyrinth, to meet what awaits us here.

—From *Communion*, by Whitley Strieber

Beads, shells, stones, broken pieces of pottery, mirrors, small found objects, fabrics, tassels, slender needles, and thin threads are materials I use to create my work. The thread in my hand explores and secures layers of individual stitches that hold the tiny pieces together.

The stitches are traditional techniques I learned from my mother when I was a child. My stitches anchor the objects down into the surface. As I hold onto the thread, I deftly plunge the slender steel needle up and down, in and out. My hand moves over the surface, pushes deep into it, and back up again. It is repetitious, and in the repetitive movements, I find I am mesmerized by the motion. In the process, I am often aware that I am walking by inner vision. When my eyes fail to guide me, my hands know what to do!

Gradually, I realize, I am painting messages from the stars with a needle and thread!

The Dreaming Prayer

Our truest life is when we are in our dreams, awake.
—Henry David Thoreau

Are you at a place in your life where you are thinking, *Now what?*

Have you lost sight of the dreams you once had?

Do you often feel like you have reached a dead end?

Maybe it seems like nothing really works out for you, or you just have no idea that life can be different than what you are experiencing at this moment. Are you feeling hopeless or unloved? Those thoughts are depressing and don't feel good, do they? You might not be where you want to be right now. This can change if you are willing to try something so simple and easy. It's really so simple you might think it would not work. But it does!

Please be patient, my friend. Learning to walk every day with our Creator is a lifelong journey. We just take one small step at a time. I am still learning every day, even after giving my life to Jesus Christ over forty years ago. Sometimes I think I am a very slow learner. But the journey with Him is one of grace and delight every day.

There are some questions to ask yourself that will help you get a better idea of what you really believe about yourself and the world you live in. They are known as "worldview" questions. If you will begin to think about them, you will soon determine where you really are in life, and they will help you gain insight as to where you are going in your future.

The best news is that you can make changes now to make your life different than what it is today. I have done this. I promise you that your circumstances and possibilities in life will change forever and for the best.

You can ask God to guide you and give you the insight you need, day by day.

What do you long for? What do you want more than anything else in your life?

Put your desire into words! The desires you have are uniquely your own. They will fit your personality and your talents. You do have a calling from God for your life, and you can find it once you begin to think about it seriously.

Are you facing a mountain that seems like it is too high to scale?

Are you in a treacherous place where you would not choose to be standing?

Have you experienced loss or failure?

Maybe it is time to make some adjustments in your life.

Do you need some divine help and guidance from God?

Let me recommend something that changed my own life many years ago. I'd like to share with you what I found one day, and it changed the entire course of my life.

The Dreaming Prayer.

This unusual prayer was first introduced by Catherine Marshall in her 1961 book *Beyond Ourselves*. Specifically, look in the book and read Chapter 11, "Dreams Come True."

Catherine's mother taught her about the Dreaming Prayer. You see, we are really on a pilgrimage all through our lives. But we don't know that. Sometimes, someone has to help us understand it. Catherine helped me to learn the Dreaming Prayer one day in the 1970s as I read her book.

We have a divine purpose in our lives. We have an inner voice that speaks to us, but we have to be quiet enough to begin to listen for it. That still, small voice is the voice of your Creator. He is speaking through the Holy Spirit, directly to you. But you have to be quiet and begin to listen. God most definitely will speak directly to you through His still small voice.

The Dreaming Prayer is a prayer of helplessness. We are asking God to help us and to set our feet on the best path of His plan for us. But, best of all, the prayer will open the windows of Heaven for us, and it is nothing but the best possible life we can imagine.

Ask God to guide you in your prayer.

You and I need help! We need to regroup.

The Dreaming Prayer will do that for you!

You will soon discover that this prayer is really all about *you*! What is it that is deep inside your spirit that is longing to have a presence in your life? Speak it out loud to God right now as it comes to your mind.

You may ask, "What if this prayer is not right for me?"
Test the prayer!

Does it fit with the scriptures in the Bible? God would never ask us to do anything that is not affirmed by His word! Seek His guidance through His word. Spend time reading the scriptures and listen for God's voice to guide you as you are meditating on His word. He will do that for you. He will speak directly to your heart, and you will know His presence in your life at those moments.

Does it benefit or edify other Christians? God will never ask you to do anything that would harm the body of Christ (other believers). Does it lift up others as well as you? Your life purpose will be a benefit to yourself as well as to those who are around you.

Expect to have some closed doors. This is often God's way of directing you to His higher purpose for your life. Please remember this: *Do not kick down doors!* That door has been closed as a providential circumstance in your life. Use your common sense and not your emotions. Stay calm when you come upon a closed door. Do not panic! It will be for the good that you would not have been able to encounter if you had walked through an open door that was not right for you.

Be sure that what you are asking for is not for God to take anything from another person to give to you! Never covet what another person has and never ask God to take away something from another person to fulfill your prayer. What God has for *you* will be just for *you*—a new thing that He has planned for your life that is yours alone.

Go ahead, find out for yourself. Go beyond yourself.

You will be so glad you took the plunge and prayed the Dreaming Prayer.

For additional information on determining your worldview, visit this link:

http://www.christianity.com/theology/other-religions-beliefs/8-questions-every-worldview-must-answer.html

NOVEMBER

Crystal Healer

Amber reds dripped from ancient trees
        solidified, fossilized
Boji Stones brought healing to painful memories,
        grounded high spiritual vibrations
Crystal quartz cleared the room of negative
        energies, brought healing to those who lost hope
Dragon's Blood was christened as costly Cinnabar
        she helped change your image
Emerald stood surrounded by palest green rays of
        light, protected from evil enchantments, foretold
        the future
Fluorite made me smile when I touched her soft
        curved celestial rainbow of clear, blue, green
        brown, and yellow
Garnet gemstones surrounded us with beauty from
        the earth, mined and carved, tumbled smooth
Hematite, a heavy magnetic stone, harmonized and
        balanced the spirit, supported timid women and
        boosted self–esteem
Iolite, small and translucent; a delicate stone,
        changed her colors with the angle of light

Jadeite, translucent, soft, and green; hidden away,
  smooth and silky in my pocket
Kunzite's delicate shades in lilac, pink, or yellow
  translucent, transparent, mood–lifting effects
Labradorite, my favorite gem, reminded me of deep
  water's reflections on a summer day
Malachite held layers of copper between her
  spiteful   greens,   powerful   stone   of   the   new
  millennium
Nebula stones are small with unique metaphysical
  properties, gaze into it, move to new places in the
  universe
Obsidian sang of a black winter night snowflakes
  falling on the shiny opaque glass–like surface
Precious opal stones, cleansed in the light at full
  moon a fiery glow, in the morning light
Quartz clusters gathered deep secrets,
  in their helical spiral crystalline forms
Rainbows flourished inside the dense earth
  a harvest of vibrant mysteries
Serpentine, a talisman of water–worn black–green
  stones, aid to assure the wearer of longevity
Tiger's Eye beads in yellow–brown, pink, blue, red,
  were used as protection against ill will
Unakite is a circus of tumbled stones
  placed gently in bowl, brought calm to your home.
Variscite sang the songs of encouragement, hope and
  courage to those who gave up
Wulfenite brings knowledge from ancient temples
  brought spiritual vibrations down to earth

X represents the signature of the Creator's hand
      as he fashioned and planted each precious gem
Yellow Calcite, my favorite stone, brought healing,
      from the darkness inside the fertile earth
Zeolite can be colorless, white, blue and peach,
      a group of all kinds of crystals, living
      together in a matrix of a harmonic rainbow.

A Wintry Tale

As I opened the kitchen door this morning, dusky light seemed to flow into the house like an old friend reaching out to greet the three of us. My daily morning ritual is a leisurely walk along the wooded ridge overlooking the creek below. Our dogs, Mitchell and Rocco, are always anxious to explore our familiar rural path, regardless of the seasonal challenges.

Rocco, our furry little Pom–Sheltie dog, is the first one that people usually respond to when they first see us. The typical comment is, "Oh, I love the little fluffy dog! He looks just like a teddy bear!" My name for him is "Fuzzy Bunny."

Rocco bounced out the door this morning into the brisk day. His long, silky tail waved in the bitter, wintry breeze, and it curled up over his back like a waterfall. He doesn't need a leash, because he understands his boundaries and he usually stays with me for our morning walk.

Mitchell is quite a contrast to Rocco as she walks beside him. She's a lean, long–legged terrier. Her short white coat looks even whiter next to Rocco's deep black-and-tan body. When people ask about her, I usually say, "She is a *terror*." Mitchell has to wear her red leather harness and stay on the leash, because she just never understands that we have boundaries. On those rare occasions when she slips out the door and runs off, she dashes around the neighborhood like a banshee flying through the night sky on Halloween Eve. She runs a race with the wind, back and forth, across the two roads near our house. She makes wide circles around every house on the road. When Mitchell happens to get loose, I see only fleeting flashes—quick explosions of a white dog darting about in ever-widening circles. She moves so fast her brown spots are invisible.

Once when that happened, all I could do was wait for her to finally come back home. In fact, once she realizes she is free to run, she never seems to recognize her name. Obviously, she has no clue that she is in danger.

This morning, Mitchell and Rocco became quite excited by the frolicking fun in the snow. They sniffed the air and looked around for fresh deer tracks. Mitchell held a pose that told me she was looking for something in the woods. She stood perfectly still, one front paw lifted up and curled in a frozen position. *It must be something big*, I thought. Her slender face and dark, red-brown eyes pointed towards the frozen, ice-covered trees. This stance always makes me a little nervous; I do not want to encounter a deer in the late fall, because the males can be dangerous. I've been chased out of the woods before, by a large buck, stomping his feet and snorting on the path just ahead of me.

I was cautious now. I knew that Rocco liked to chase a deer deeper into the woods if he had the opportunity to do it. On several previous occasions, after a chance meet–up with a wild deer, Rocco immediately began to chase the deer. When he finally returned to me, his long–haired body trembled with excitement. But today, no deer in sight. Mitchell soon began her sniffing, and we kept going on our path.

On wintry mornings when snow covered our landscape, crisp air was pierced by the loud calls of a lone crow gliding high above the tops of the trees. A couple of cars drove by on the main road as we stomped through the wet snow. Finally, we three early morning travelers turned around and headed back up the hill to the house. It always looks magical to me, because it is a black house. Each time I stop to think about it, I feel like it hovers at the top of the silvery, snow–covered hill. I often feel like I'm walking in a dream or in the mythical land of Narnia, where it is perpetual winter. That image makes me smile, because I love winter. The dark house ahead of us gave me a warm feeling. I walked with my thoughts focused on the beauty of this day.

I must have looked especially strange, because I wore my tall, rubber "wellies" to get me safely through the deep snow drifts. Since this is a rural area and no one would see me walking through the woods, I was also wearing my long, lavender flannel nightgown under my purple plush bathrobe instead of a winter coat.

Suddenly, frisky, impulsive Mitchell jerked me into the center of a snowdrift that was higher than my boot tops. My flannel nightgown caught the snow as the three of us launched into the drift. Heavy snow surrounded me with shocking wetness against the bare skin above my boot tops. My bathrobe flapped in the wintry coldness that blew up from the creek bed.

I tried holding up my snow–laden nightgown, but the snow blobs stuck fast. Icy snow clung all around the inside hem of my flannel nightgown as I plunged on down the hillside into the meadow on the ridge overlooking the frozen creek. I was a human bobsled, plunging swiftly down the hill.

I barely recall the short second I felt my right boot slip beneath the snow and I was thrown down onto my face with my hands extended outward above my head. My legs apart, the toes of my wellies dug into the drift, thrusting my face deeper into the snow. Mitchell quickly turned around to see what was happening when she felt the leash pull her to a stop. Fortunately, I held tight, and was still laughing as I staggered back up onto my feet.

It happened so fast, I could never have prevented this fall. It was painless. I began to laugh out loud. I hoped my husband was not watching from the window. I did not want him to see our morning plunge into the newly fallen snow. But my desire for secrecy was soon shattered when my husband greeted us at the kitchen door. He was laughing, and so was I. We laughed together as I realized he had seen me rolling out of control, head down, as if I was a fast-moving sled pulled by a frantic white dog. I was completely covered with snow. I giggled as I came through the door and announced, "Here come the snow bunnies!"

The Dragon's Healing Breastplate

It is by going down into the abyss that we recover the treasures of life. Where you stumble, there lies your treasure.
—Joseph Campbell

For where your treasure is, there your heart will be also.
—Luke 12:34

Photography, an interest and passion for me since I earned my first camera by selling Girl Scout cookies, remains a focus to this day. From childhood to the present, I am seldom without a camera nearby. I've captured some memorable photographic images with my camera. I'm inspired by the landscape and nature at any time of day, in any season. But in my imagination, there are even more distinct and vivid photos I collected from the stories I read through my lifetime romance with literature. Each story is a snapshot of people, place, and time.

In my memoryscapes, I stand as a witness where I observe some special women who show details of their lives in a unique slice of time and place. Each woman has a connection with a divine presence, and each has some aspect of the fiber arts at the center of her story. The women's stories were passed down from antiquity via oral tradition and writings by historians. The texts from different cultures at various time periods give us insight and inspiration for living a meaningful life in our own time and place. The women in the writings add valuable information that will enlighten or help contemporary people to understand timeless universal truths. The imprint of the past cannot be erased. It won't disappear, but remains with us through the generations.

I'm innately aware of the perpetuity of traces that human history has left behind for all of us to discover. It's imperative that I look for the layers of history's traces in order to fit together the pieces of the enigma of our individual life story. At times, I have a sense that I am walking over layers of ancestors, walking in their footprints, listening to their voices, learning about life's meaning directly from them. In my being, I hear the voices from the "world without end." I listen.

In each of my favorite stories, there's a remarkable woman who saves the lives of other people, or she brings healing through the creative use of fiber arts, such as thread, yarn, weaving, embroidery, or working with precious beads and stones.

Storytellers of early Greek mythology introduced me to a young girl named Ariadne. The vivid picture I have of her in my mind is unforgettable. In the Greek worldview, there are humans, like you and me, who are mortal. We will live our lives, grow old, and die. As a contrast, in Greek and Roman myths, we encounter supernatural gods, goddesses, and mythical, magical creatures that are immortal. Many of the unusual hybrid creatures in myth originate when an immortal has a sexual encounter with a mortal.

Ariadne was an immortal. She was a beautiful young woman who stands in my imaginary photo with a ball of red thread in her outstretched hands. In the mythological tale, Ariadne was the daughter of King Minos of Crete. He was the son of Zeus. His queen, Pasiphaë, was the daughter of Helios. Ariadne, of course, was a royal princess in an immortal family of the gods.

As in many other myths and folk tales, immortal Ariadne fell passionately in love with a strikingly handsome young mortal man. Theseus came from Athens; he was visiting Crete at this time. It so happened that seven youths and seven maidens were required to be sacrificed to the Minotaur, a vicious creature—half bull and half man. The legendary Minotaur was kept in a maze called the Labyrinth. As the myth unfolds, we learn that the fourteen young victims were randomly selected to be sacrificed periodically (some sources say it was every year, another says every seven or nine years) in order to appease the gods who had brought a plague upon Crete. Theseus was a youth who volunteered to kill the Minotaur. He and the others would enter the Labyrinth, where they would be devoured by the Minotaur. No one who entered this lair ever found a way back out again, because the maze was so complex. It was designed and created by two gods; therefore, once a mortal stepped inside it, they were doomed.

The twist in the story is that Ariadne was in charge of the Labyrinth where the sacrifices were made.

As Theseus was about to go into the Labyrinth, Ariadne gave him a sword and a ball of red thread. He walked through the complicated Labyrinth slowly and unrolled the ball of thread. He found the Minotaur asleep in the center of the maze and he killed it with the sword Ariadne had given him. Theseus followed the trail of red thread to escape from the Labyrinth, and all the others who had entered with him came out safely, as well.

In my imaginary photo collection of heroic women, there is another who stands with a scarlet cord in her hand. We find the story of Rahab in the Old Testament Book of Joshua (second chapter). The time period was when the Hebrew people were just entering into the Promised Land. Two spies were sent into Jericho to scope out the city and the people in advance of the coming invasion of the Hebrews. The two spies encountered Rahab, who spun and dyed flax on the roof of her home. Her house was built into the city wall.

> *"(18) Behold, when we come into the land, you shall tie this scarlet cord in the window through which you let us down, and you shall gather into your house your father and mother, your brothers, and all your father's household. (19) Then if anyone goes out of the doors of your house into the street, his blood shall be on his own head, and we shall be guiltless. But if a hand is laid on anyone who*

is with you in the house, his blood shall be on our head. (20) But if you tell this business of ours, then we shall be guiltless with respect to your oath that you have made us swear." (21) And she said, "According to your words, so be it." Then she sent them away, and they departed. And she tied the scarlet cord in the window.

Rahab placed a scarlet cord that she made in the window, and it hung down over the outside wall of the city. The cord was a signal to the men who would be coming to destroy the city that this house was not to be touched. Her house would be passed over, and everyone inside the house marked by the scarlet cord would be spared when the moment arrived for the destruction of the entire city to begin.

These stories, found in historic texts, compel me to ask:

"What is there about a piece of spun fiber, such as a red thread or a scarlet cord, which is significant enough to guide Theseus through a complex maze in Greek myth?

"Or why was a woven cord used as a sentinel to warn and protect a home and its inhabitants, as it did with Rahab?"

In both stories, there was an impending danger that threatened the lives of the women and their families and a significant life–altering change that occurred. The red thread and scarlet cord are symbolic images that pivot events and bring a triumphant victory in the lives of both women. Both thread and cord provided a way out of disaster for the people in the stories. They also provided escape from imminent death in both stories.

I offer here a final glimpse into a personal memoryscape, involving my own life experience at a time of crisis and uncertainty. In this picture, I hold in my hands an object that appears to be a talisman from the ancient past. A talisman is a protective garment or piece of jewelry that is worn to ward off evil spirits, defeat enemies in battle, or bring healing, energy, and clarity to the mind of the one who wears it. A talisman is a sacred object.

It is an art work I created at a terrifying time, a life crisis. This tale is not from antiquity, yet the images, metaphors, and influences are clearly present. These noble women served as guides in my journey through uncharted territory. The most notable aspect of the talisman, which I call "The Dragon's Healing Breastplate," is that this art work marks the end of my sighted life and the beginning of my life of profound sight loss.

"The Dragon's Healing Breastplate" is a mixed–media fiber sculpture. It has the appearance of an ancient necklace that would be worn by royalty. It looks like some sort of ceremonial neckpiece with a dragon image as the center of interest to signify the importance of the person who wears it. It is not really a wearable adornment, but a clever deception.

This encrusted beadwork "showstopper" is what I label "Unwearable Art," and it holds a special place in my own personal life journey.

In my academic lectures and research articles, I have always had a keen interest in studies of ancient and medieval mythology and imagery. The many parallels I discovered between contemporary culture, our daily life, and the historic stories from the past led me to devote my research inquiries to new discoveries and revelations.

While on a trip to New York City in August 2007, I purchased the beads and central dragon image that I planned to use in a new project. What I did not know on that sunny August afternoon was that I would not be physically able to bring it to completion as I anticipated.

Shortly after I started work on this piece, I suddenly lost most of my eyesight. With only one fourth of the piece completed, it came to a screeching stop. I could no longer see the piece at all and had no way of ever knowing if I would be able to do this kind of intricate bead working in the future. I plunged into despair at times, yet I always kept this dragon image in my thoughts. I longed to be able to create such magical, inspired work again.

After five years of adjustment to my new life, and with the help of significant blind rehabilitation, I returned to this work to pick up where I had left off. I can tell you, it was not an easy task. I experienced many frustrating failures, tangled messes of thread and beads, and discouraging mistakes before I finally reached the place in my mind where I had the confidence to be able to work again on this piece. Just as the dragon image in ancient Eastern culture is one of healing and protection, this particular dragon became a healing symbol, or trophy, to me. The dragon signaled that, just as Rahab did so long ago, I had won the battle and beaten the doubts. I rejoiced in the victory of my own return to wholeness. The mixed–

media fiber object, the dragon image, is symbolic of my own creative journey and healing. Creating this piece of art connected me with confidence in divine guidance and a deep understanding that I intuitively share healing through my artworks.

I ask myself, "What do I see when I look at this artwork?"

I view a picture of an inner landscape; it shows the terrain inside the Labyrinth of my own inner struggles. Inside this complex maze, I can visualize a creative path that required new visions. Ariadne's ball of red thread and Rahab's scarlet cord are a powerful metaphor; it connects and guides me.

Some days, I move forward in my chair as I sit in my office and write stories or create poems. Other days, I hold tight to a slender needle with thread in my hand. I've researched the time and place in which my slice of story occurs. Willfully, I walk into the mists of the unclear, uncharted chronicle.

The final snapshot: Rahab, Ariadne, and me. We stand together in this place. Here is where our eyes see glory!

Notes

Joshua 2:1, 3; 6:17–25; Matthew 1:5; Hebrews 11:31; James 2:25.

Meaning of Rahab's name: The first part, *Ra*, was the name of an Egyptian god.

Rahab was an Amorite who lived in Jericho at the time of its destruction.

DECEMBER

And the Word became flesh and dwelt among us, full of grace and truth; we have beheld His glory, glory as of the only Son from the Father.

—John 1:14

Christmas Scentiments

All I want for Christmas is aroma therapy
beneath my fragrant Christmas tree.
"Chanel #5" casts a festive spell. I want it!
Did I mention I'd like some kick–ass shoes, too?
expensive Italian shoes suit me best. I want them!
Forget about those elfin gifts
get me Ferragamo, size 8 in soft brown leather.
handbags from Italy? yes, I want Sharif.
I admit I am a handbag snob—I want gifts from Paris, too.
just give me what I want and nothing less.
keep shopping till you drop, Dear Santa!
let me give you additional tips for what I want
Marilyn Miglin's "M" perfume, Versace "Crystal
Noir" (with never–ending desires)
or "Opium" to send me into "Euphoria."
"Pheromone" is an exotic fragrance—I want.
QVC is a great place to shop for scentiments—I can't
resist ordering an extra bottle or two!
"send me the most expensive bottles," I say!

These days, even Santa's reindeer shop online
up on the housetop the team takes a break
Vixen and Prancer order bottles of toilette
water for sweet–smelling girls like me!
"X–O–X–O–X" Kisses and hugs for you! Oh, remember
Yves Saint Laurent makes delightful scents but, I almost
    forgot—I want
"Zen White Heat," the best Christmas Scentiment of all.

Signed: With never–ending desires, I'm your girl! Lynda

A Western Pennsylvania Christmas

"Oh, it is so cold this morning! My lips are probably blue! Are they, Patti? Are my lips blue? I don't want to get up," I whimpered.

My sister and I shared a bedroom. Patti woke up now because I was complaining. She took a deep breath, then she spoke slowly, "Do we have to get up already?" She took a quick look towards the wall of double–hung windows on her side of the bed. "It's still kind of dark outside," she announced. A cold wind was blowing outside.

Just like every other house in the neighborhood, ours was a typical home like those of most of the steelworkers in our little city. The wood–frame house had a wide porch that spanned the front of the house from one side to the other. The front door was in the center of the porch, with a large window on each side of it.

Mom was proud of the organdy ruffled curtains in every room of the house. They were a lot of work for her, and it was even harder because of all the soot that drifted in on the air from outside.

"Just a couple more days till Santa comes," Mom said. School would be closed soon, and we would be home for the Christmas holiday.

Our two-story house was heated by a large coal furnace two floors below our bedroom. The cast-iron furnace stood like a hulking giant right in the center of the hard dirt floor of the basement. Its round, hollow arms captured heat from the furnace and moved it upwards into the entire house. Dad got up before dawn to get the fire started. Once the fire was giving off heat, Dad could leave for his walk down the railroad tracks, across the creek, to the steel mill. Dad made stainless steel. In winter time, he left in the dark morning and returned home in the dark evening.

Coal, the central part of our lives, heated our homes in the 1940s. The coal miners of western Pennsylvania provided coal needed all across the country.

Homes and factories were no longer heated by wood. Coal was the king of daily life in America since the late 19th century in the northeastern United States. Pennsylvania coal was needed for homes, steamships, locomotives, and factories. Children growing up in western Pennsylvania knew a lot about coal.

Every home had a coal furnace, a coal chute, and a coal cellar in the basement. The black dust filled the air all through the basement and outside on the day when the coal truck made its delivery.

Mom's voice sounded urgent. "Girls! Are you out of bed yet? You better be up, because we have to leave soon, and you need to have your breakfast first. Your oatmeal is ready. Come and get it before it gets cold!"

Patti and I both decided to jump out of bed at the same time. Our bare feet hit the highly polished pine floor as we jumped down from the bed. We were wearing our flannel nightgowns. With a rush in the brisk morning, we ran the few steps from the bed to the registers in the bedroom. "Oh, the register feels so good," I said. We huddled together, each of us trying to keep our cold, bare feet on the warming metal register in our bedroom floor.

Two floors below our bedroom, Dad had the fire blazing. When he was certain it was going to keep on burning, he closed the heavy cast iron door. Dad knew how to keep the fire burning for hours at a time. My awareness of the magic of coal and fire was in those daily trips to the basement to watch Dad work the fire into a frenzy. Dad was a magician, and we four children were his attentive audience as he practiced daily magic rituals.

One afternoon, we all sat around the long mahogany table in the dining room together. Santa needed letters from us so he would know what we wanted for Christmas. We had the Sears catalogue, and we all gathered around it to get a look at all the delights on the pages of the catalogue.

"I want a Snow White doll. She comes with her seven dwarves, too! I really, really want a Snow White doll," Patti cooed with determination.

The two boys were mostly interested in some new trucks and cars, like the red fire truck with ladders and the solid metal green bulldozers and tractors they saw in the catalogue.

We all wanted to be certain Santa got our lists, so we wrote down our favorite toys.

Coal is a shiny black rock. I actually know it is magic, because a piece of coal burns. A rock that burns! Bituminous coal is also called "soft coal," and it starts to burn much more quickly than the other kind of coal. The other kind of coal is anthracite, and that is usually called "hard coal."

The biggest problem we all had was the dirty soot that gathered on our porch and windowsills. Soot blew into the sky from the steel mills. It was greasy, black little fragments that floated in the air and landed on all the houses and porches. Cleaning the porches and windows seemed like an endless job to us when the weather was warmer. When winter came, the snow would get a layer of the black dust all over it.

"Have you written your letters to Santa yet?" Dad asked.

"Yes," we all said at the same time.

Since I was the oldest, I was in charge of getting things done in the house. I handed Dad the four lists we created. We had written them on our school tablets, with the blue lines on the white paper. We were all aware that it was getting close to Christmas, and we four were all anxious to get those letters off to Santa.

I felt a little nervous about my letter, though, because I knew I had not been good sometimes during the year. I was thinking about the fight we had in the summer. I recalled how the neighbor sent all three of us children home when she heard us fighting in her yard. Santa might know about it, and then I would be in trouble with the gifts, I realized. And how did Santa know everything? Well, that is simple. It is the elves he sends out to spy on us. They report back to him when they see us doing things that are not so nice. When I thought about it, I could remember some other naughty things I did that year.

When we wrote the letters to Santa, my brothers kept watching out the windows for elves, too. Mom told us often during this time of year about the elves watching us day and night. It was frightening to think about it, really! Terror filled our hearts because we all knew the penalty that we would receive on Christmas Day. We had been warned again and again about the dreaded gift we could receive if we had been bad!

I really wanted to get a travel alarm clock, like the one a classmate brought to school one day. My classmate seemed to have everything; I was so jealous of her. But her little red travel alarm clock was the best Christmas gift I could imagine, so I wrote that in my letter to Santa. As I wrote about the travel alarm clock, though, I began to remember that I had stolen some colored pencils while another student was outside for recess. I hoped it would not count because I had to give them back to her after the teacher found out.

I was also thinking about the night our littlest brother played with matches, and how he set the glider in flames. He was really in trouble for that, but it turned out okay because we put the fire out with a bucket of water.

I also remembered the fight I had with our neighbor girl. We got into a fist fight, and I pulled her hair. I wondered if the elves had seen us that day in our little hideout in the field, as we fought like wildcats.

Dad opened the furnace door, and the fire felt like it was going to come out and burn us up. "We will put the lists in the fire now. Santa will get your list, because he will read the smoke from the chimney."

We watched as the paper curled up quickly, caught on fire, and turned into nothing as the fire consumed it before our eyes. Dad closed the door with a clank that startled us back to the moment.

I am not sure if those smoke messages really did get to Santa, though.

On Christmas morning, we opened our gifts. There were some cars and trucks, teddy bears, and even an erector set. Patti's new Snow White doll did have a box full of dwarves with it, just as she had asked for in her letter. *Santa got it right,* I was thinking.

I was excited as I held the square package that was just the right size for the travel alarm clock. It was a thrill to even think about what I was going to find inside that wrapping paper. I ripped it off, and there was my gift! A musical powder box! But I never wanted a powder box at all! What was Santa thinking about when he picked out this gift for me?

It was only a few minutes before another even bigger disappointment came that really spoiled my day. Santa had filled our stockings just like he said he would. I was nearly finished opening them when I saw one final package for me. It was a bit heavy for such a small package, too. Once again, I had a burst of renewed energy and got excited with the anticipation of something that I would love to get from Santa. As I ripped the red shiny paper off the gift, my hopes turned to despair.

Oh, no! This is the worst thing that can happen, I thought.

Now I knew for sure the elves had done their sneaky job in reporting misdeeds to Santa for the entire year. I held out my hand and slowly turned the lump of coal around in it for everyone to see. That day I learned a truth that every kid in western Pennsylvania knows. The good little children get gifts that are nice, and the naughty ones get a lump of coal in their Christmas stockings! Santa was for real!

End Note

Work in the mines was hard and dangerous. Between 1877 and 1940, 18,000 men and boys died in Pennsylvania bituminous mines.
—PA Coal History
http://explorepahistory.com/story.php?storyId=1-9-18

A Meditation on the Angel Candle

Do not be afraid; for behold, I bring you good news of great joy which will be for all the people; for today in the city of David there has been born for you a Savior, who is Christ the Lord. This will be a sign for you: you will find a baby wrapped in cloths and lying in a manger.

And suddenly there appeared with the angel a multitude of the heavenly host praising God and saying, "Glory to God in the highest, and on earth peace among men with whom He is pleased."
—Luke 2:8–14

When a celestial messenger appeared in the Biblical story of the birth of Jesus, we immediately knew that something miraculous was happening.

An angel visited some shepherds who were out in the fields at night so that they could watch over their sheep to protect the flock from predators. The visitation from an angel was completely out of the ordinary, and the shepherds were frightened. But the angel quickly told them, "Fear not!" This angel was sent to make an announcement that would change the lives of humans forever.

In modern times, many Christians make an Advent wreath for their homes as a central part of their celebration of the birth of Jesus. On the wreath, there are four purple candles around the outside of a circle of pine. The circle is symbolic of the eternity of God. Christians light one candle a week prior to Christmas day.

The first candle stands for Hope. The second candle signifies Peace. Candle three is for Joy. And candle four is for Love. It's also known as the Angel Candle.

After the lighting of the Angel Candle, there is one final white candle that is in the center of the Advent wreath. It is the Jesus Candle, and it is lit on Christmas Day.

Just like that first announcement in the fields near Bethlehem, music and celebration of the Holy Birth are an integral part of our Christmas traditions as we consider the miracle of Christ's coming into human hearts. We, like the shepherds in the dark fields, can turn around one day and answer God's call to "Fear not!" as we hear God's quiet invitation to change our life.

There is comfort in knowing that angels are still with us during challenging periods of our life journey.

In the angelic Christmas message, we can continue to live our lives in expectation of the miraculous. The weekly candle lighting during the four weeks of Advent reminds us that God is still in control of our world. Because of the gift of His son to the world, we can receive His eternal gifts of hope, peace, joy, and love through the birth of our

Savior, Jesus Christ. Fear not!

Come to Me, all who are weary and heavy–laden, and I will give you rest. Take My yoke upon you and learn from Me, for I am gentle and humble in heart, and you will find rest for your souls.
—Matthew 11:28 (NASB)

Fear not!

The Living Room

A baby on its mother's back does not know the way is long.
—African proverb

Esther looked forward to the one special night of the year when she wouldn't be lonely in her quiet home. She walked slowly through the stillness and then stopped briefly to look out the large picture window in her spacious living room. She checked once again to see if anyone had arrived yet. She wouldn't be alone tonight because it was Christmas Eve. Every year, Esther's four grown children returned home with their families to celebrate this special evening together. Esther's face would be radiant with happiness throughout this evening, and she would be transformed into the queen of the night. Esther was the lone matriarch of the family.

That night, the elongated living room would quickly fill up with her children, grandchildren, and even great–grandchildren. The room was built with enough space for holding large gatherings for all sorts of family events.

Along the one long wall, there was a gray stone fireplace. As she had done for many years previously, she had decorated it with her hand–painted ceramic angels. The three elegant angels were glazed all over in pearly white. Each carried a different musical instrument. She had accented those instruments with a glittering gold paint that matched the halo on each angel's head. She always placed cranberry–red candles among the angels and carefully arranged boughs of pine across the mantle.

The graceful holiday decorations created shimmering reflections in the wide mirror that stretched out the entire length of the mantel behind them. The reflections made the room seem joyful and optimistic as the little multi–colored twinkle lights flashed brilliantly around the edges of the mirror. When Esther's husband, Bill, was still alive, he always made a crackling fire in that fireplace. Now it was bare and unused. She did not turn on the stereo tonight because she did not think about it.

For this special occasion, Esther selected her favorite Christmas sweater. She wore it at Christmas for years. The bright holiday sweater made her feel happy. It was a warm sweater in bright Christmas red, and on the front it had white poinsettias and golden ribbons woven into the fabric. She didn't think about what her two sisters would probably be wearing when they arrived tonight.

The two elderly women, Fanchion and Bettie, arrived early in the evening, and as usual, each lady wore a noticeably similar Christmas sweater. The three sisters always shopped together, and most of the time, when one sister selected something to buy, the other two bought one just like it.

The siblings often grumbled about each other, but they went shopping together often. Shopping helped fill the emptiness of their long days. The sisters each lived separately, in their own homes. They lived about two miles apart. They came from a family of seven children. At this time, only four girls survived. They had lost the two brothers and one sister in the last decade.

Esther did not think about them very often anymore. Sometime she even forgot they were no longer living and seemed surprised when someone mentioned they had passed away. She would become agitated; her eyes would widen as she said, "They died? Oh, no! I didn't know that. Why didn't you tell me they died? I wanted to see them again! I wanted to go to their funerals. Why didn't anyone let me know about this?"

Each time she learned again that one of her siblings was dead, she wept all over again. It always happened when someone brought up a conversation about their deaths. Each time, it was the beginning of grieving for her.

When Esther's children looked back through old family photos, they laughed when they saw the three sisters sitting at a wedding reception. Each sister was dressed in a delicate little flowered dress. Very often, another sister, Jeanne, was there in the photos, and sometimes her outfit looked like the other sisters' clothing. Strange, wasn't it? They all had the same taste.

In the final decade of their lives, Esther, Fanchion, and Bettie lived alone, but they did many things together.

Fanchion's husband died at a very young age. They

had two teenage children when he died. She was on her own after that. She worked in a neighborhood bakery. Everyone in town knew her from the bakery. Her two children left home to go to school in different states, and they never returned to the small, rural town where Fanchion and her sisters lived.

Fanchion's two children lived far away. After Christmas each year, Fanchion flew across the country to visit with her son for a month. When she returned from her annual winter visit in sunny California, she spent the rest of the year telling stories about her visit.

Bettie's name was actually Mary Elizabeth. In infancy, she had a kidney disease, and the family gave her special attention because she was so sick. After her retirement, she spent every day with her older sister, Fanchion. Bettie worked as a secretary in the local steel mill, where she was hired right after she graduated from high school. Throughout her long life, she told stories about her travels across the country in her girlfriend's new car. Her long trip to California and her one–time trip to Jamaica with her girlfriends gave her memories to talk about for the rest of her life.

Esther's husband, Bill, died eleven years before this night. It happened suddenly one Saturday morning. It was in July. While Esther prepared their breakfast in the kitchen at the opposite end of the home, Bill left this world. He was in their bedroom and had not yet come out to have his breakfast with Esther. His sudden departure was a shock she never really recovered from.

I recall several occasions when she grew silent, and it

was apparent she was overcome with sadness as she spoke. I turned my head away, for her words were too hard for me to take in. I tried to hold back my own tears as I silently inhaled and held my breath.

"I never even got to say goodbye to Bill. I realize he hasn't come out of our room yet. I am in the kitchen, reading my morning devotions. I hear him get up and go to the bathroom. Then, I think he should have come out for breakfast by now. Where is he? I walk through the living room and into our bedroom. He is just lying there on the bed. All stretched out on his back. His arms are wide open, and his feet hang down, almost touching the floor. He is wearing one sock but the other foot is bare. I see he was putting on his socks. But he's not moving. I scream and rush over to him. I shake him, but he never moves. I try to put my mouth over his open mouth, and I try to breathe into him to wake him up. Nothing is working. I leave him and I run as fast as I can run, through the house, out the door, across the lawn to the neighbor's house. I need help! Bill needs help; he isn't breathing and I cannot wake him up."

Bill left Esther alone at 6:30 a.m. on July 17, 1988. This is the year they would have celebrated their fiftieth wedding anniversary, on Christmas Day!

Esther was now seventy–nine years old and still a beautiful woman. Her sharp, deep, amber–brown eyes had clouded over. They looked like a gray film had grown over the rich darkness of her eyes. She was still tall and looked stately. Her dark, raven hair had slowly transformed into a soft silver color and was now short. She patiently watched out the thick glass window at the end of the living room.

"I am sure someone will be here soon," she whispered to the empty living room.

Some people told Esther she should sell her house and move into a smaller one. They said she needed one without such a big yard to take care of since Bill wasn't there anymore. Her four children spoke about this to each other, and once in a while, one of her children told her she needed to move out of the big house so she would not have so many things to worry about and such a large yard that needed tending. But Esther's response to everyone who said something like that was, "No, Bill built this house, and I can never leave it. And, if I sold this house, we would not have a place for our Christmas Eve party."

Esther was stoic in her determination to stay in the home she helped build. She managed to hold onto her home because it was built just for her, and she loved it. The walls of every room surrounded her with a lifetime of memories. And it held future possibilities for her Christmas Eve parties for her family.

Bill and Esther did build the house they planned. When they were younger and their four children were all at home, Esther and Bill dreamed about the house they would build someday. Bill, a good artist and draftsman, entertained the children with his drawings of cartoons and animals. He made sketches of the ideas they formulated and envisioned their new house. Each of the children could recall the many times their parents pored over plans for the new home they wanted to build. Bill even constructed a meticulous scale model of the house they planned together. The model he built was large. It was on a sheet of plywood. Bill spent the long, solitary winter months in the basement working on the model. One of the features they planned so carefully was the spacious living room. It was the most important room in their home.

Now, so many years later, Esther was here all alone inside their dream house. They had worked side by side to build this home. Esther was thirty–eight years old and Bill was forty–two when they moved their young family of four children into this house. It was the house where the children grew up together.

Esther and Bill always dreamed of living in a nice neighborhood and in a house that they built. They made their dream come true. It was a little at a time, as they could pay for the things they needed when building it.

Bill was a Pennsylvania steelworker. I can remember so many times when the men who worked in the steel mill went out on strike or when there would be layoffs, and those times were difficult for our family. After they started building the house, there would be several times when all construction work came to a standstill due to unemployment. Our whole family actually moved into the basement of the house. I was fifteen years old that summer. While our family lived in that basement, the upstairs was being built. In a year or so, we all finally moved upstairs into the newly finished house.

It was exciting for me, as a fifteen–year–old girl, to be part of this new adventure in our life.

It was a sultry, warm summer day, and the men were there to start mixing up the fresh batches of plaster. They set up all the equipment outside the front room, right there in the mud. They laid down some boards, and they walked back and forth on the boards, pushing the wheelbarrow. Some of the men were carrying the wet plaster on large boards. They held the boards up with one arm and balanced it on a shoulder and walked as fast as they could towards the house. They were really strong men, and this was hard work, carrying all the plaster into the house and to the room where they were putting it on the walls. With each trip into the house, the men started to cover the open studding. They were making wet walls that were getting thick and strong. I liked to hang around watching the men and joke with them a lot.

When they came that day, I told them, "I want you to make the plaster lavender for my bedroom."

The man looked at me while he shook his head from side to side. "We never made lavender plaster before, but I'll see if we can figure out how to do it."

I looked at him and offered one final plea for lavender plaster. "I really want lavender plaster in my room! It's my favorite color, and I don't want anything else but lavender."

It was not long before the crew began carrying in the lavender plaster for my bedroom.

I have to share this new room with my sister, Patti, and I hope she likes lavender, because that is just what we are getting, I thought.

I did not mention the fact that Mom had told us that once the room was plastered, we could go pick our fabric for the new drapes she would order. I told her, "I'm going to pick out fabric that has a black–and–white abstract print on it."

Our long–awaited new house was completed over the next week, as the laborers made trip after trip from the mixing place outside into the rooms inside the new ranch–style house.

I have always loved real hand–crafted plaster. The walls seem so solid and give me a feeling that I am safe inside of them. When I rap on a real plastered wall, I can hear the dull thud that does not make an echo. The house seems to have a nicer voice once it is dry and has aged. The older it gets, the clearer it sounds. Handmade plaster sounds soft and friendly. When I lay my ear beside those walls, I can listen to the men talking as they carried the plaster and slathered it onto the walls. I can hear the men bring in the plaster and the sounds of my two brothers and my sister as we danced about inside the bare, unfinished house. Memories whisper to me, and I can hear the many voices from the past. The plastered walls have the power to speak, and the voices of our family remain inside the plastered walls.

One of the loveliest sounds that echoed through the house was Esther's voice as she sang hymns. She was a strong singer with a ringing alto voice. The living room was her concert hall as she dusted the tabletops or washed the large picture window.

Esther Luella Kirker started singing as a small child with her family. Almost her entire family sang or played a musical instrument. Everyone who knew her family always remarked about the music they all made together at the local Methodist church. Esther's father, James, played the coronet in the church orchestra. Her oldest brother, Clair, was there, too, because he played the tenor saxophone. Sister Jeanne played the piano. Esther sang along with the family musicians. Her voice was her instrument. Esther sang at church. Members of the congregation often asked her to sing their favorite hymns. She continued singing those old–time heavenly songs by memory her entire life.

My mother had forgotten many things, but she never forgot how to sing. She never forgot the words or the melodies of the old hymns. "How Great Thou Art" and "In the Garden" are two hymns that still ring in my memory today. I remember my mother's voice.

Around 7:00 p.m., everyone began to arrive. They parked on the blacktop driveway at the Mercer Road residence. Cars soon lined the driveway and even down the sides onto the frozen lawn. All our family members came bursting through the front door. They called out, "Merry Christmas!" and laughed as they greeted each other with hugs and smiles. They carried in holiday foods wrapped up with foil, and they juggled boxes and bags of brightly wrapped gifts. Each person wore holiday outfits for this special night. Christmas Eve at our house was a grand affair, and everyone always dressed in their sparkling new outfits. Velvet, lace, silk, and taffeta dresses were on all the little curly–haired granddaughters. Their little brothers had slicked–down hair, and they arrived with small metal model cars and soft, stuffed toys to keep them busy.

Once our family members began arriving with their

arms stacked with wrapped gifts and foods, we quickly put out the colorful holiday food on the table Esther had prepared for this feast. Esther served the very same punch every year. It was a fruity punch, and we all expected to enjoy it. If she ever changed and used a different recipe, it would not be the same for us. We loved her frothy, pink fruit punch. When my father was still living, I brought him his favorite pie, an old–fashioned shoo–fly pie or a mincemeat pie. For all the others, I baked pecan pies and praline pumpkin pies.

Dad was a smoker most of his life. He used to laugh and say he started smoking when he was ten years old. When times were hard and the mills were on strike, Dad always rolled his own cigarettes at the kitchen table. Mom just hated smoking. We children liked the smoke rings. Dad sat down in his rocking chair, tilted his head back a little bit, and made his mouth into an "O" shape. He liked to blow those smoke circles into the air. He entertained us with those magical rings of smoke dissipating into the atmosphere of the living room. As he sat in his favorite chair blowing smoke rings, we giggled. When one of the kids had an earache, Dad blew smoke into the painful ear to bring relief.

Eventually, Dad did his smoking outside, since our mom didn't want smoke in the house. He went on long walks in the woods. I think he took those long walks so he could smoke all he wanted to with nobody to tell him he should not be doing it. He had a contrary spirit and he liked to do things that made other people angry, sometimes.

What I liked best about his walks in the woods was the variety of mushrooms he brought home for us to eat. He soaked the wild mushrooms in salty water to clean them. The next thing he did was put them in a sizzling skillet and fry the sweet, earthy fungi in butter. Oh, I can still taste those freshly gathered, tasty treats!! Bill knew the woods and he knew exactly where to go to find the different kinds of mushrooms. How I wish I had learned how to hunt for mushrooms with him!

After Bill's meals, every day, he made his favorite dessert. It was a "coffee soak," as he called it. He took a couple of pieces of bread and put them on his plate. Then he poured hot coffee over the bread and added a nice, generous scoop of sugar to the top. The sugar soaked up the coffee and melted into the bread. Every meal ended with that treat for Bill. The kitchen had a warm coffee aroma as Bill enjoyed his coffee soak.

When the new house was nearly finished, Bill brought some spindly trees home from the woods. He planted them around the house and down the driveway. One neighbor remarked, "Those trees from the woods will never grow." This night, the bare winter branches of the maple and sycamore trees stand tall and strong in the early darkness of a Pennsylvania winter. They are just like my father and mother might have imagined them forty years earlier. Our father's hands were hardened by years of labor in the steel mill, yet he carefully crafted this house and the surrounding beauty of the yard through years of sacrifice and labor.

Tonight, in the gently beating heart of our family

home, our mother's swollen, arthritic hands struggle to open the gifts that are stacked around her. She looks so fragile and seems almost like she is drifting away to another place while we sit and watch her surrounded by her unopened gifts. These days, she struggles with almost everything. She often forgets ordinary things she has done for many years in earlier times of her life. She does not say very much tonight, but she keeps on smiling. It is almost like she is part of a dream. She is like a Christmas angel, surrounded by her many offspring. She is quieter tonight. Sometimes she looks lost in the middle of the family celebration in the living room. At times, I watch her and try to imagine what she might be thinking about in the middle of this noisy laughter.

The plastered walls of this living room are filled with our memories of parties, wedding showers, dancing feet, laughing children, praying, intimate embraces, our father's smoke rings, our mother's songs, and sorrowful tears.

As I glance over at her, I wonder if she is listening to the walls, hearing the voices from the past years. Esther looks out over the five generations who have gathered here every Christmas Eve. The annual photos record the changes in the family. Small babies who once crawled on the floor now bring their own little babies to squirm through the ocean of wrapping paper. Bill is no longer in any of the family Christmas photos. Esther looks frail, and smaller than she does in those photos.

The living room has now become a witness in the house we filled with laughter, tears, and secrets. The living room is part of a conspiracy tonight.

We all know that this Christmas Eve gathering is Esther's last Christmas Eve party in her home. We will never again be here as a family gathered around together. We are all facing a shift in our lives. We will all be going in different directions after this night. While we smile and chat, we are lonely and deeply sad. I wrote a special poem about the house and gave a copy of it to every family member tonight. There are tears behind our smiles. We all feel the meaning of the word "bittersweet."

Epilogue

The day after Christmas, I took my mom to the local hospital for an evaluation. As we had all suspected, she was diagnosed with advanced Alzheimer's disease. She lived another eight years, but we would never again be in the living room of our childhood home for another celebration. This was the end of all our happy holidays together as a family. Our mother's life changed, and so did we. Each Christmas Eve, the living room remains the same as we always knew it. But now, it is only in our memories.

Morning Prayer:
In Which I Learned to Blossom

And the day came when the risk to remain tight in a bud was more painful than the risk it took to blossom.
—Anaïs Nin

Eventually it happens. We begin to think about universal questions asked by every human being from the beginning of recorded history to the present moment.

Who am I?

Why am I here in this world at this precise time?

What is my purpose?

For a large part of my life, I accepted the idea that my art and writing life was separate from my spiritual journey. During years of rigorous academic studies, there had never been a dialogue that addressed fundamental questions concerning my creativity in connection to my personal faith and theology. I never questioned or explored my worldview. Well, in fact, I didn't know I even had a worldview. During the nine years of full time studies to earn three degrees, this concept never came up in any classroom discussion, so I kept my personal faith walk private.

As a new professor, I arrived at the college where I would begin my career as a tenured professor. My title was Professor of Fine Arts and Humanities. It was thrilling for me to see my name and title on a golden plate on the door of my new office. My classroom duties began at the beginning of the fall semester. This time period is the beginning of the academic year.

Initially, I faced a challenge because the core philosophy of this college is the integration of faith and learning. That meant I was expected to teach every course in such a way that my Christian faith would be central to my teaching. How would I integrate my Christian faith into my classroom courses? How could I find synthesis between academic pursuits and "integration of faith and learning"? All my previous academic training and research in higher education left me in a quandary about how I would accomplish the mission of the college, for the universities I had attended were completely secular. Even though I thrived in my studies, there was a part of my human self that formal education never addressed. Worse yet, I was unaware of the gap. Part of me was missing, and I never realized it. We are a tripartite being, yet the spiritual part of our humanity is seldom, if ever, addressed during our years of higher education, unless we attend a private university with a Christian worldview.

Thus, my quest for discovering how to present a personal Christian presence in my professional, academic, and creative life began. Prior to beginning my new job, I thought of my life as being divided into two boxes—sacred and secular. With the dynamic new teaching adventure, my entire life was turned upside down; it seemed I was in a tailspin! I had to find the way to bring faith into my discipline, but my years of training and practice left me confused about the possibility of this marriage.

When I began this exciting new position, I accepted the idea that my art was separate from my personal life story and my spiritual journey. Rigorous academic pursuits had never led to a dialogue that addressed fundamental questions concerning my disciplines in connection to my personal faith and theology. Religious convictions were kept private, quiet, never to be uttered in academic discussions. Dozens of courses are listed on my transcripts, yet not one addressed the notion that I had a purpose in life or a calling from God.

My timid prayer one morning was a request that God would guide me in this new pursuit to allow Him to be in my classrooms and with me in my lectures. I surely had no idea how this could possibly happen. This new concept haunted me as I tried to plan out my daily course activities for each class. Integration of faith and learning was on my mind continuously. I had to figure this out; it felt like the strangest request I had ever made for divine help. This was a crisis for me, and I surely needed help so I could be in partnership with my colleagues and students. Gradually, I came to realize that my personal life, my own history, and creative activities are not at all separate. Each is part of my own tree of life. With the discovery that my Christian roots run deep and were planted in good soil, the tree of my own life flourished. I was a whole, complete person bringing the truth of the ages into my professional life in my classrooms.

I always embraced the idea of being a lifelong learner, and that propelled me to develop my distinct teaching style. Along with my students, we began to piece together the human puzzle. I asked the Worldview Questions in my studio art classes, researched them in our humanities courses, read deep into them through literary discussions, dug into our collective history, listened to the music from all time periods, and read the philosophy of inspired men and women through the ages. Together, professor and students discovered layers of connections between our individual creative work, our academic aspirations, personal and cultural history, and the Christian faith. The most remarkable discovery I made is that there should be no line that separates teacher from students. And, beyond that discovery, I learned there is no line separating the secular from the sacred in this world. I learned to be a servant leader. And, I learned to bloom!

With every passing year, I continue to see how large the world is and how it is ever–expanding and changing. The entire universe stands as a witness to the creative powers of an intelligent mind. We can find the presence of a Creator God in every aspect of the creation.

Though I retired from my formal work in a variety of classrooms and lecture halls, I am still a lifelong learner. Presently, my lifelong passions of making art and writing are still at the center of my days. My exhibitions of art continue as I gather awards, and my artworks still appear in galleries and museums across the U.S.

Most days, I am either in my fiber art studio working on a new piece, or in my office writing about the significance of our life journey. My art and my writing convey the timeless message of who we are in Christ. My studio and my office are light–filled rooms where I encounter glory. I walk into one of the rooms and ask God, "What would you have me do today?"

Soon, the work on my new book, *Walking by Inner Vision: Stories & Poems,* will be completed, and the book will be sent to the publisher. But I won't be suffering for lack of something to do, because my thoughts contain a rich bounty of stories and poems and more books, like tight buds waiting to unfold.

As with most transitions in life, inspiration begins as a tiny seed planted deep in the mind. I envision life changes as a little, fluttering butterfly swooping across a flower garden, gliding on the breeze on a warm summer day.

Our life is a blossom dancing in the moment on a gentle breeze as the Holy Spirit orchestrates the music. We dance together in divine harmony.

About the Author

Life is either a daring adventure or nothing. To keep our faces toward change and behave like free spirits in the presence of fate is strength undefeatable.
—Helen Keller

Lynda McKinney Lambert
Visual Artist, Author, Educator, Blogger

In her first book, *Concerti: Psalms for the Pilgrimage* (Kota Press, 2003), Lynda invites readers to begin a pilgrimage through poems, historical notes, and journal reflections written during her summers in Austria and other European countries. This publication marked the beginning of her literary journey that continues with the publication of her work in numerous books, blogs, and literary journals.

Walking by Inner Vision: Stories & Poems continues the pilgrimage as she gives readers a glimpse into a private world of limited sight. Lynda suddenly lost most of her eyesight in 2007. However, it is not a world of lost vision, imagination, or insight.

Lynda has no central vision, which means she cannot see details or colors. She has limited peripheral vision that is cloudy and gray. She describes her vision as similar to walking in a winter snowstorm at twilight.

Lynda's themes emerge from decades of multilayered life experiences. Her lifelong interest in history, fine arts, and literature gives her writing a firm foundation on which she weaves a tapestry of contemporary reflections.

A pilgrimage is an individual path for each person. Yet it is also a universal passage. Just about everything in our shared human experience requires adaptation and adjustment to change. We can revise!

Lynda McKinney Lambert holds a BFA degree in painting and an MA degree in English from Slippery Rock

University of Pennsylvania, and an MFA degree in painting from West Virginia University. She is now retired as a professor of fine arts and humanities at Geneva College in western Pennsylvania.

Note

For additional information about her availability for presentations at conferences, hospitals, civic organizations, and university classes, please contact her by email: riverroad@zoominternet.net

Lynda McKinney Lambert
104 River Road
Ellwood City, PA 16117

Lynda's personal website:
www.lyndalambert.com

Lynda's book–related website:
http://www.dldbooks.com/lyndalambert/

Lynda's three Facebook pages:

Walking by Inner Vision blog:
https://www.facebook.com/walkingbyinnervision/

SCANdalous blog:
https://www.facebook.com/SCANdalous–Blog–782814908467623/

River Road Studio:
https://www.facebook.com/River–Road–Studio–175785105811956/

E–mail:
riverwoman@zoominternet.net
llambert@zoominternet.net
riverroad@zoominternet.net

Acknowledgments

Grateful acknowledgment is given to my best friend and husband, Charles Robert (Bob) Lambert, for inspiration, support, encouragement, and dedication. You never allowed me to quit; you led by example.

With unconditional love to my children:
Salomé Lambert Mengel; Heidi Lambert McClure; Victoria Lambert Jacques; Ilsa Lambert Barry; Robert Andrew Lambert.

With deep appreciation to the organizations that have shown me how to regain my creative life as a person with profound sight loss:
American Foundation for the Blind
American Printing House for the Blind
Art In–Sights exhibitions, Louisville, KY
Behind Our Eyes writers' group
Blind and Vision Rehabilitation Services, Pittsburgh, PA
Hadley Institute for the Blind and Visually Impaired

Keystone Blind Association, Sharon, PA
National Federation of the Blind, Writers' Division
Pennsylvania Bureau of Blindness and Vision Services, Erie, PA

Grateful acknowledgment is made to the editors of the following journals and anthologies in which these creative nonfiction essays, poems, journal entries and memoirs appeared.

Amy's Adventures blog, by Amy Bovaird:
    "Kaleidoscope: Patterns of Light and Dreams"

Concerti: Psalms for the Pilgrimage, by Lynda Lambert, Kota Press, January 1, 2003:
    "Excerpt from a Journal Entry, July 8, 1999"
    "Notes from the Baroque Museum," journal entry, July 21, 1999
    "Slowly, Suddenly: Remembering Persephone"
    "Two Friends on a Bench"

The Consumer Vision online magazine:
    "A January State of Mind"
    "From the Other Side of the Mountain"
    "When I Begin my Day with Mozart"
    "A Visitation from Butterflies"

Dialogue Magazine, Blindskills, Inc.:
    "Knitting a Life Back Together"

Exceptions Magazine: The Art and Literary Journal for Individuals with Disabilities, Spring 2016, Michigan State University:
 "Muddy Hands"
 "Girl on a Bench Sees Visions of Butterflies"

Expanding Visions, Women's Caucus for Art, Washington, D.C., 1991:
 "Summer Story"

Indiana Voice Journal:
 "A January State of Mind"
 "When I Begin My Day with Mozart"
 "A Visitation from Butterflies"
 "Girl on a Bench Sees Visions of Butterflies"
 "Musings on 'E'"
 "The Connie"
 "Great–Grandmother Speaks"
 "Crystal Healer"

In Other Words anthology:
 "Sunday Morning in Winter"

Light Magazine, Christian Record Services, Sept/Oct 2015:
 "When I Begin my Day with Mozart"

Magnets and Ladders literary magazine, published by Behind Our Eyes, Inc.:
 "Adornment: September Daydreams"
 "Christmas Scentiments"

"In Which I Find Color in Late Winter"
"Muddy Hands"
"Musings on 'E'"
"My Daughter Cut the Roses"
"Notes from the Baroque Museum"
"Silver Cloud Dancer"
"Try to Capture September"
"Two Friends on a Bench"

Spirit Fire Review:
"Prologue: In Which I Knit a Life Back Together"

SCANdalous–Recollections blog:
www.llambert363.wordpress.com
"A January State of Mind"
"Gestures"
"I Believe in Angels"
"In Which I Find Color in Late Winter"
"Kaleidoscope: Patterns of Light and Dreams"
"March Arrived Like a Capricious Cat"
"My Daughter Cut the Roses"
"The Connie"
"The Dreaming Prayer"
"The Living Room"
"Visitation from Butterflies"
"When I Begin my Day with Mozart"
"When the Bear Goes over the Mountain"

Stylist (a.k.a. *Slate & Style*) *Magazine*, NFB Writers' Division:
    "William's Red Roses"
    "The Living Room"

Walking by Inner Vision blog:
www.lyndalambert.com
    "Adornment"
    "A Visitation from Butterflies"
    "A Western Pennsylvania Christmas"
    "A Wintry Tale"
    "Crystal Healer"
    "Gestures"
    "I Believe in Angels"
    "My Daughter Cut the Roses"
    "The Connie"
    "The Morning Hour"
    "The Poetry Ladies"
    "Try to Capture September"

Wordgathering
    Volume 10, Issue 4, December 2016:
    "Star Signs"
    Listen to "Star Signs," read by Melissa Cotter:
    http://www.wordgathering.com/issue40/poetry/lambert.mp3

Editing and Publishing Assistance

This book was proofread and edited by David Dvorkin and Leonore H. Dvorkin, of Denver, Colorado. David designed the cover and did all the technical work required for the publication of the book.

David and Leonore are both much-published authors, with numerous articles and over 30 books, both fiction and nonfiction, to their credit. Four of those books are by Leonore. Her memoir, *Another Chance at Life: A Breast Cancer Survivor's Journey*, is available in e-book, print, and audio formats, as well as in Spanish. The 2012 edition is the most recent one.

Since 2009, David and Leonore have been working to help other authors self-publish their books. Most of their editing clients are blind or visually impaired.

They invite you to visit their websites for full details of their services, the books by their clients, and their own publications.

DLD Books: www.dldbooks.com
David Dvorkin: www.dvorkin.com
Leonore H. Dvorkin: www.leonoredvorkin.com

75714119R00134

Made in the USA
Columbia, SC
27 August 2017